Christendom
Revisited

BOOKS BY JOHN A. GATES
Published by The Westminster Press®

Christendom Revisited: A Kierkegaardian View
of the Church Today

The Life and Thought of Kierkegaard
for Everyman

Christendom Revisited

A Kierkegaardian View of the Church Today

by
John A. Gates

Philadelphia
The Westminster Press

Acknowledgment is made for permission to quote from the following:
Christian Discourses, by Søren Kierkegaard, tr. by Walter Lowrie. Oxford University Press (London), 1939.
For Self-examination, by Søren Kierkegaard, tr. by Edna and Howard Hong. Augsburg Publishing House, 1940. (Paperback)
Attack Upon "Christendom" and *Training in Christianity,* by Søren Kierkegaard, tr. by Walter Lowrie. Princeton University Press, 1944.

PUBLISHED BY THE WESTMINSTER PRESS®
PHILADELPHIA 7, PENNSYLVANIA

PRINTED IN THE UNITED STATES OF AMERICA

To
Luther A. Weigle

Contents

Preface

IT HAS BEEN three years or more since one of the editors of The Westminster Press encountered a statement of mine to the effect that the extremes to which Kierkegaard went in his criticism of the Danish Lutheran Church of his day should not obscure the fact that basically these criticisms were just and that most of them apply to the church in our day also. The last clause of the statement was parenthetical, but it gave this editor an idea. It would be possible to apply Kierkegaard's categories of criticism to the contemporary American church in a book that would be authentically Christian and would also be publishable. So the editor said to me, "Why don't *you* do it?"

In my initial naïveté the project appealed to me. As I have pursued it, however, I have had mixed emotions. It is not easy to criticize one's friends, and many of my most valued friends are my fellow ministers. It is not easy for me to write devastatingly about the church—an institution that has nurtured me, provided me with the vocation that gives greatest meaning to my life, and to which I will always be bound by ties of affection and conviction. So—for three years I have worked off and on at this thing, all the time dragging my feet. My editor has not pushed me unduly; but my conscience has. I had never intended to write such a book, I did not want to write it, but I have felt that I must.

In the writing, I have experimented with various types of format, one of which would have been a Kierkegaardian *Journal*, written as though he himself were observing the American scene. I gave this up for two reasons: (1) I didn't think I had the literary skill to do it well; and (2) I decided it would be an evasive attempt to appear to avoid personal responsibility for what I was writing.

The book is an essay in unfairness. Quite deliberately it will be a one-sided presentation of the situation of Protestant churches and ministers in the United States. But the facts will be facts, and the statements made will be true, to the best of my knowledge and ability, even though some persons will, perhaps, think them a caricature of the truth.

The church today is highly vulnerable. There are so many chinks in its armor that one who is probing for them does not have to seek far or with unusual diligence. Faults of the church peer from every pew, and pontificate from every pulpit. Ordinarily, people do not see them; or, if they do see them, they are so accustomed to them that they take them for granted. If perchance churchmen do talk about the faults of the church, it is a sort of defense mechanism which they use to excuse themselves for their own hypocrisies.

At any rate, the church is characterized today by a vast and ignorant complacency. It is my purpose, as it was Kierkegaard's, to disturb that complacency. Others are doing this, and doing it well. I am not here attempting to duplicate their efforts, or to produce a comprehensive critique of the church. I have limited myself to the Kierkegaardian categories of criticism. These are, in my judgment, authentically Christian. While Kierkegaard's all-out attack on the Danish Lutheran Church of his day took place in the last year of his life, 1855, and is published in English as the *Attack Upon "Christendom,"* S. K. began laying the groundwork for the attack in the second and third parts of his book *Christian Discourses,* published in 1848. The thesis, with which he began rather subtly in this work, is that Christianity is a redemptive faith to be sure, but it is also a demanding faith. It is the failure of Protestantism that it has not made the demanding aspect of Christianity plain to men. This comes out clearly in Part III of the *Christian Discourses:* "Thoughts Which Wound from Behind," and is an increasingly prominent theme in *The Sickness Unto Death* (1849), *Training in Christianity* (1850), *For Self-examination* (1851), and *Judge for Yourselves* (1851–1852, but unpublished in S. K.'s lifetime). After more than two years of silence, the theme bursts forth in a thunderous crescendo in the *Attack.* There is also much material in Kierkegaard's *Journals* that satirizes the triviality and hypocrisy of conventional Christianity.

The idea of Christendom—a segment of the world's population and a section of its land area in which everyone is a Christian—was S. K.'s broadest and most all-inclusive target. It is still a current and widely held idea. It is, indeed, a civilization—a culture, a social order—Western society, if you will. It is Christian only in the very loose sense that it is broadly informed and infiltrated by Christian ideas. It is Christian in the same sense that the United States is spoken of as "a Christian nation," and the United States is a Christian nation in approximately the same sense that Kierkegaard's Denmark was Christian one hundred years ago. It is the current American version of Christendom at which we are now to take an unjaundiced (I hope) but incredulous look.

On one occasion, when I had discussed the plan for this book with a college class in philosophy, a student came to me afterward with the suggestion that I entitle it "Christendom Revisited." As Wordsworth returned to Tintern Abbey, and as Aldous Huxley has much more recently returned to his "Brave New World," so Kierkegaard would be given an opportunity, in spirit, to revisit Christendom.

Other titles have been considered and rejected; this one has survived. It is, to me at least, an intriguing title, and indicates fairly clearly what I have hoped to do with the book. It is also a presumptuous title; for I am not a Kierkegaard, and can never hope to recapture the vigor and immediacy of his nineteenth-century *Attack Upon "Christendom."* I feel quite humble about this, as indeed I have felt about the whole project from the beginning. I think of myself as a reluctant intermediary, a somewhat unwilling human channel of communication between a nineteenth-century genius and twentieth-century mediocrity. I am painfully aware that I share this mediocrity, and that I do not in any way approach Kierkegaard's genius.

I am also deeply convinced, however, that what I am saying here "has to be said; so be it now said" (*Attack Upon "Christendom,"* p. 59). I am grateful to many persons who have helped, and especially to my editor for his initial suggestion and for his encouragement along the way. The idea was his; the ideas are Kierkegaard's; whatever truth the book may contain is of the Holy Spirit; the mistakes and the responsibility are mine.

J. A. G.

Westminster College
Fulton, Missouri

CHAPTER ONE

Christianity or Christendom

WHEN, in 1855, Søren Kierkegaard launched his attack upon the Lutheran state church of Denmark, he took his stand on the solid ground of Biblical faith. Christianity, properly so called, is not a product of human culture but a revelation from God. The New Testament, which is the climactic stage of this revelation, draws a sharp line between the church and the world. The Christian is to live a life of love in the world, but he is not to embrace the world as his way of life. His goals of achievement and his guidelines for decision are provided by the truth made manifest, and the love revealed, in Jesus Christ.

Christianity is primarily personal; it is the authentic context for the relationship of an individual human being to God. This relationship must begin in what Kierkegaard called an "infinite resignation." The Christian individual professes and deeply feels his willingness to give up for Christ's sake everything the world counts valuable. If God requires it of him, he will give up children, home, friends, position, property, even life itself. Becoming a Christian is an act of the individual human will. It is a loving, grateful surrender of all that one is, or hopes to be, to a God whom one trusts completely.

13

Indeed faith—this complete trust in God—is a necessary element in surrender. Infinite resignation and trust, together, constitute what Kierkegaard called "the infinite double movement of faith." The man of faith will live in complete acceptance of, and obedience to, God's will because he trusts God completely.

There is, of course, a further and more compelling motivation for the personal act of faith by which one becomes a Christian. One becomes willing to surrender to God because, when he relies on himself in the struggle with evil, he loses most of the battles. Even when one thinks he is earnestly trying to do the right, if he is honest with himself he knows that he doesn't succeed on his own power. One becomes willing to surrender his life to God, not only because he trusts God, but also because he distrusts himself. He cannot prevent himself from sinning, and yet he feels responsible for his sins. He is beset by complex feelings of guilt, inadequacy, and helplessness. In despair of himself, he finds in the Christian gospel a message of hope and a way of strength.

He is aware that God is righteousness and cannot condone sin. But this same God has also revealed himself in Jesus Christ as One who became man in order to free men from the power of sin. God's infinite, forgiving love does not contradict his infinite righteousness; each is in the deepest sense an expression of the other; and both are his chosen channels for expressing his infinite power and wisdom in his relationships to finite man.

This is the God whom the Christian accepts and loves, and to whom he is willing to surrender his life in utter trusting obedience. When one has willingly done this, it then becomes his task to discover what obedience involves in his own particular situation. It is, in general, clear that he is to express God's love in human relationships. He accepts his place and responsibilities in the world without letting the world determine his inner life of the spirit—his motives, attitudes, purposes.

It is no easy thing to be in the world but not of it. The world (i.e., society) is the necessary medium of civilized living. It has its place in the providence of God. Its mores are to be respected, and many of its folkways may be enjoyed. It can be, and usually is, for a normal human being, a structure of meaningful relationships. For the Christian, however, the world is not ultimate. It can be a theater of worthy and significant activity. It has its claim upon him for services rendered. It cannot command his supreme allegiance. His citizenship is in heaven, and his primary group relationship is to the family of God— the redeemed community, the church.

In New Testament times and for several generations afterward, Christians rather typically understood this tension between the church and the world. To be sure, persecution of the church by worldly powers made their separateness obvious. Separateness, however, was not the result of persecution but its cause. The church would not have been persecuted if the conflict of ultimate loyalties had not already been made clear by the refusal of Christians to put Caesar before Christ. For the early Christians the church and the world stood in clear antithesis.

The recognition of Christianity as the official religion of the Empire by the Roman emperor Constantine has been acclaimed as the conquest of the Roman world by Christianity. What really happened, Kierkegaard says, is that Christianity was conquered by the world. There was no longer any tension between Christianity and society. Christianity became acculturized. The line that had once been clearly drawn between church and world became vague and tended to disappear. Christians gradually became "naturalized citizens" of a society that had its roots in this world.

Indeed, as this process of acculturization continued, it became the accepted thing in Western society for a man to be regarded as a Christian. In medieval times almost everyone was assumed to belong to the church, the membership of which was coterminous with the secular state. In fact, the state was no longer secular. It became theoretically an adjunct of the church, and the empire in western Europe was revived as the *Holy Roman Empire*.

The almost complete accommodation of Christianity to culture was a gradual development, and from time to time there were voices of dissent. The Protestant Reformation was, indeed, an effective reaffirmation of Biblical faith. It brought the Bible back to the people. It made many changes in the direction of the Christianity of the New Testament. But it failed to separate Christianity from Western culture. By and large it left the common man, in the Lutheran sections of Europe at least, without any ability to distinguish between the commands of God and the mores of society. Even the Protestant clergy in Denmark seemed to have no clear idea that there was any such distinction. Christianity had been swallowed up in a pseudo-Christian colossus which men in western Europe called Christendom.

It was against this false figment of men's imaginations, and its consequences, that Kierkegaard leveled his attack. It is a concept that rests upon the assumption that those lands in which Christianity is either the established or the predominant faith are "Christian nations."

These Christian nations as a group constitute Christendom. A corollary of this false assumption was an even more grievously false assumption that all residents of Christendom are, per se, Christians.

Kierkegaard points out in his *Concluding Unscientific Postscript,* and frequently in subsequent writings, that anyone who was a resident of Denmark and had been baptized, regardless of the life he was leading, was a "Christian."

> But if a man were to say quite simply and unassumingly that he was concerned for himself lest perhaps he had no right to call himself a Christian, he would indeed not suffer persecution or be put to death, but he would be smothered in angry glances, and people would say: "How tiresome to make such a fuss about nothing at all; why can't he behave like the rest of us, who are all Christians?" . . . And if he happened to be married, his wife would say to him: "Dear husband of mine, how can you get such notions into your head? How can you doubt that you are a Christian? Are you not a Dane, and does not the geography say that the Lutheran form of the Christian religion is the ruling religion in Denmark? For you are surely not a Jew, nor are you a Mohammedan; what then can you be if not a Christian?" (P. 49.)

It is easy for us to smile at the provincialism and naïveté of folk religion in nineteenth-century Denmark. In the United States in this third quarter of the twentieth century, we are more discriminating and more sophisticated. We realize that (excluding the population of foxholes in World War II) there are some atheists. We take it for granted that in our country a man is free to be faith-less, religiously speaking, and some individuals exercise this freedom. We would also recognize that many professing Christians make no pretense of living up to the ideals they have professed.

We are, however, in our own way, grievously confused. We point with pride to the tremendous wave of religious interest in the United States since World War II. Statistics tell us that almost two thirds of the American people are now church members. Indeed, the ratio of church members to the general population has risen fairly steadily in this country since 1890; and this rise was especially rapid in the years between 1940 and 1960. (Claire Cox, *The New-Time Religion,* p. 14; Prentice-Hall, Inc., 1961.)

It is true that these figures are highly inaccurate. However, our interest in them is not statistical. They do indicate a trend and a state of mind. It is proper and popular to be religious. There have been many hallelujahs on the part of the not-so-thoughtful church leaders because of this "surge of piety." They forget that from the time of Constantine on, popularity and a mass influx of "converts" have been disastrous for Christianity. The more "Christians" there are, the less Christian they are.

It is not exactly more difficult to be a Christian when everyone around you also bears the label, but it is much less likely. There is an insidious corruptiveness about worldly approval. The false prophets of whom our Lord speaks (Luke 6:26) originally, perhaps, meant well. They simply became *false* prophets "in response to popular demand." The Christian should be warned when all men speak well of him, and there is, possibly, a greater danger of this in the United States today than at any time in Christian history.

This is because American society has become a reasonable facsimile of what S. K. meant by his use of the word

"Christendom." We are a religious nation. Will Herberg has shown this with all needed supporting evidence in his book *Protestant—Catholic—Jew* (Doubleday & Company, Inc., 1955). Herberg calls attention to a paradoxical situation: a growing religious interest and a growing secularism, which exist side by side, not only in American society, but also in the thought patterns of individual Americans.

For example, it seems reasonable to assume on statistical grounds that a majority of the thirty outstanding Americans who were asked to rate the one hundred most significant events in history were professing Christians. Yet in their poll they rated first the discovery of America by Columbus. Gutenberg's invention of movable type was second. Eleven events were tied for third place; and the crucifixion of Christ was tied with five other events for fourth place, really fourteenth, since thirteen other events were rated as more important. (Herberg, *op. cit.*, pp. 13–17.) Obviously these eminent Americans did not take their religion seriously. As Herberg comments: "The secularism that pervades the American consciousness is essentially of this kind: it is thinking and living in terms of a framework of reality and value remote from the religious beliefs simultaneously professed." (*Ibid.*, p. 14.)

This is the nature of Christendom, that millions of its "inmates" give lip service to a faith in which they do not really believe, and which they do not understand or even want to understand. The "Christian" faith of most Americans today is no less naïve, and no less mistaken, than that of run-of-the-mill Christians in mid-nineteenth-century Denmark. Indeed, all indications would lead us to conclude that it is more ill informed, more mistaken, and farther from the truth.

The folk religion of Christendom in the nineteenth century was immersed in the sort of self-indulgent error and intolerant tolerance to which human nature is always prone. But most people in the mid-nineteenth century were still fairly close to the world view of the ancients. They could more readily share the perspectives of the universe and man that prevailed in Bible times and are implicit in the writings of the Bible. Increasingly, after the middle of the nineteenth century, scientific developments, universal education, and the thinking of leading intellectuals changed the whole climate of popular thought. Man was conceived and described in evolutionary and materialistic terms; and the universe, in terms of inexorable natural law and illimitable space. We in our generation in America are the inheritors of these changes in man's total frame of reference. The ongoing processes of our society—industrialization, urbanization, scientific medicine, increasing automation even in our homes, growing mass conformity, comfort, convenience, speed, and greed—have made us a deeply secular, if not indeed a materialistic, people. It is extremely difficult for persons immersed in the mores and folkways of such a society to maintain any sense of spiritual reality or of the importance of spiritual values.

The world "has come of age" and confronts Christianity with what may prove to be a greater challenge than any it has previously met. Added to the factors of self-indulgent human nature and urgent social conformity that have long operated to produce the nondescript monster which Kierkegaard called Christendom, we now have these inescapable changes in men's thinking, which are of the nature of *our* society.

Some Americans still have a sense of spiritual need. The statistics of church membership do not prove that we are Christians, but they do, perhaps, indicate that millions of people in our materialistic civilization know that they lack something. The fusion of the church with the world—the confusion of Christianity with culture—can never supply this lack or meet this need. Christendom is a whited sepulcher, a misleading caricature of Christianity. It is a broken cistern that can hold no water. It promises what Christianity has to offer without charging the price that an honest Christianity must demand. Christendom is a fraud.

Christendom is displayed in many features of program and activity of American Protestant churches. These must be subjected to critical reexamination and radical revision if the church is to be Christian, and if its members are to be Christians. This will be the burden of subsequent chapters.

CHAPTER TWO

Our Religious Establishment

THE LUTHERAN CHURCH OF DENMARK was, and is, an established church. It was supported by Government funds; its important appointments were involved in governmental as well as ecclesiastical politics; and the laws of the state made it difficult for a citizen to be anything but a Lutheran (unless he was a Jew). Some of Kierkegaard's most biting satire and bitter invective were directed against this thorough prostitution of church to state. "Official Christianity," says Kierkegaard, cannot be the Christianity of the New Testament. He put this very succinctly in his pamphlet of May 16, 1855:

> The official worship of God (with the claim of being the Christianity of the New Testament) is, Christianly, a counterfeit, a forgery.
>
> But thou, thou plain Christian, . . . art entirely bona fide, confiding in the conviction that everything is all right, that it is the Christianity of the New Testament. This forgery is so deeply ingrained that doubtless there even are priests who continue to live on in the vain conceit that everything is all right, that it is the Christianity of the New Testament. For really this forgery is the counterfeit which came about in the course of centuries, whereby little by little, Christianity has become exactly the opposite of what it is in the New Testament. (*Attack*, pp. 59–60.)

To Kierkegaard the priests of the Danish Lutheran Church were state functionaries. Their ordination oath to interpret the Scriptures faithfully was in direct conflict with their acceptance of support from and resulting responsibility to the secular state. To be a priest in such a situation was a disobedient attempt to serve two masters. A comic aspect is that when the priest takes his official oath to interpret the Bible faithfully, he takes it upon this book which expressly forbids the taking of oaths. In Kierkegaard's day an established church was the general rule in nearly all countries of Europe. The state church, Catholic or Protestant, was supported by tax funds. In Protestant countries, particularly, there was a considerable degree of Government control. The Government-supported church was not a free church.

In societies where church and state were so closely related—"amalgamated," Kierkegaard says—the illusion of "Christendom" was very strong. Where everyone is magically made into a "Christian" by law, we may expect other, and equal, absurdities.

> I venture . . . to go a step further, . . . and hence submit to persons well informed, the specialists, the question whether among the domestic animals, the nobler ones, the horse, the dog, the cow, there might not be visible some Christian token. . . . Just think what it means to live in a Christian state, a Christian nation, where everything is Christian, and we are all Christians, where, however a man twists and turns, he sees nothing but Christianity and Christendom. . . . It is not unlikely that this may have an influence upon the nobler domestic animals, and thereby in turn upon that which, according to the judgment of both the veterinary and the priest, is the most important thing, namely the progeny. Jacob's cunning device is well known, how in order to get speckled lambs he laid speckled rods in the watering troughs, so that the ewes saw nothing but speckles and therefore gave birth to speckled lambs. It is not

unlikely—although I do not presume to have any definite opinion, as I am not a specialist, and therefore would rather submit the question to a committee composed, for example, of veterinaries and priests—it is not unlikely that it will end with domestic animals in "Christendom" bringing into the world a Christian progeny. (*Ibid.,* pp. 105–106.)

It is indeed comic that men should suppose that there can be a Christian state, or that Christianity, truly so called, can be advanced, sustained, or witnessed to by the support of the state. What the civil government is concerned for, and rightly, is public order, and the moral and material welfare of its citizens. The responsibilities of the public official are legislative or administrative, or have to do with law enforcement. If the official is a Christian, these become Christian responsibilities. Christianity had its beginnings and has continued to function within the framework of the social order. In this sense we can say with Paul, "The powers that be are ordained of God" (Rom. 13:1, KJV). This is Scripture and the clear teaching of New Testament Christianity.

However, while the New Testament recognizes the important place of civil government, it does not confuse citizenship in the state with Christianity. The Christian faith is deeply personal. It is a voluntary, consciously accepted relationship between individual human beings and God. One doesn't become a Christian by biological or social inheritance, but by personal surrender and commitment. By virtue of this commitment and by the power of his redemption through Christ, the Christian is a citizen primarily of a heavenly Kingdom. Secondarily (but necessarily) he is also a concerned and responsible citizen of an earthly society—a city, a nation, a human political and social group, a culture. His heavenly citizenship is structured by his membership in the church, which is primarily a divine institution—a colony of heaven in an alien land. The two citizenships are not completely extricable, but they are centered in two clearly distinguishable frames of reference.

For church and state to be amalgamated has historically, in Protestant countries, meant the subordination of church to state. The church can be itself only as it is free of all external control.

There are many reasons why Americans are committed to the principle of separation of church and state. It is not our purpose here to give a reasoned argument in defense of this principle. By and large, with some disagreement as to details, it is held to be a sound and desirable arrangement by nearly all Americans. The Constitution of the United States has, since 1791, forbidden the Congress to make any law "respecting the establishment of religion or forbidding the free exercise thereof." The Constitution also provides that "no religious test shall ever be required as a qualification to any office or public trust under the United States." These provisions of our basic law are regarded as forbidding the use of tax money for religious purposes. In general we Americans congratulate ourselves that we have escaped the evils inherent in a state church and an established religion.

But have we escaped these evils? The practice of having an established church still continues in Denmark and also, for example, in Great Britain. In spite of this, it is quite possible that Danes and Britons are freer to worship God as they choose, or not to worship him at all, than are respectable middle-class Americans. Americans are legally quite free in religious matters, but the very absence of legal strictures has somehow resulted in the development of social pressures. These social pressures are not only potent, they are popular, and Mr. Average American does not even want to resist them.

Religion in any society becomes a part of the fabric of that society. It provides motivation, justification, and integration for much that is typical in a culture. It sanctions mores and, perhaps, even folkways. Over a period of many generations, a religion that began as a transforming force tends to become a force for conformity, and to be itself conformed to patterns of society that are essentially secular if not pagan.

This has happened in the United States to the degree that, as Herberg points out, "The American system is one of stable coexistence of three equi-legitimate religious communities grounded in the common culture-religion of America" (*op. cit.*, p. 275). Subtly but surely the point of view has become widespread that not to be Protestant, or Catholic, or Jew, is somehow not to be an American. Nearly all Americans think of themselves as having some affiliation or alignment with one of the three "religions of democracy." So it is that when a man is obviously not a Catholic or a Jew, he is regarded by himself and others as a Protestant. This creates some amazing and amusing situations. It is reminiscent of Kierkegaard's "Christian whoremonger" who, in order to get a license to operate his unsavory business, had to profess on his application that he was of the Lutheran faith.

These comic discrepancies are not the most serious consequence of the wholesale religiosity of a society. There has also resulted in America a vast ambiguity concerning what it means to be a Christian or a church member. Some aspects of this ambiguity will be discussed in later chapters. Our present point is that the average local church of Protestant vintage has become an agency valued, even by most of its members, for its service to the community in general, as well as for its services to its members in particular.

Each particular church fits into its own groove in the social structure of the community. Protestantism has been accused of being a middle-class group that excludes and neglects the working class. For Protestantism as a whole this is not true. In 1945-1946 the Office of Public Opinion Research at Princeton conducted a survey for the Federal Council of Churches. The following chart, cited by Herberg, is a statistical summary of this research with reference to economic groupings. (*Op. cit.*, p. 241. See also *Information Service*, Federal Council of Churches, New York, May 15, 1948.)

	TOTAL	UPPER	MIDDLE	LOWER
National Sample	100.0%	13.1%	30.7%	56.2%
Protestants	69.0	13.8	32.6	53.6
Catholics	19.9	8.7	24.7	66.6
Jews	4.5	21.8	32.0	46.2
Others	6.6			

There has probably been an improvement of the economic status of American families since 1946, so that the lower class is now smaller, and the middle class correspondingly larger. This, however, does not invalidate the statistics for our present purpose. It would appear, therefore, that Protestants, constituting 69 percent of the total population surveyed, are represented in each economic bracket in proportions closely corresponding to the figures for the general population. Roman Catholics, on the other hand, are underrepresented in the upper group and overrepresented in the lower, while Jews are overrepresented in the upper group and underrepresented in the lower. These figures would indicate that

Protestants are not exclusively or disproportionately a middle-class group.

This is not the whole picture, however. There is a vast difference in the social stratification of Protestant denominations. Episcopalians, Presbyterians, and Congregationalists showed a distribution closely corresponding to that of the Jews, i.e., they are predominantly upper- and middle-class churches. Baptists, on the other hand, are (in this one respect!) like Roman Catholics. They have a disproportionate representation in the low-income group. The low-income Roman Catholics are largely city dwellers, however, while the low-income Baptists are largely rural. (Herberg, *op. cit.*, pp. 229, 241–242.)

An analysis of education levels revealed similar differences. Thirty-six percent of Baptists were high school graduates, 43 percent of Catholics, 49 percent of Protestants as a whole, 63 percent of Jews and Presbyterians, and 65 percent of Episcopalians. Catholics were predominantly urban, Jews almost entirely so.

Herberg does not mention the Holiness and other sectarian groups, but it seems safe to assume that they would rank lower in the economic and educational scales than Baptists or Roman Catholics. It is also clear, I think, that at the grass roots level, particular congregations, being Episcopalian, Presbyterian, Methodist, Baptist, or "Church of God Holiness," and not just Protestant, will have a membership approximately corresponding to the class distribution of these denominations in general. The uniformity of this denominational pattern would, however, be materially affected by the character of the neighborhood in which urban and suburban churches are located. In any case, our particular churches are to a considerable degree class churches.

The social and residential patterns of the American people being what they are, this is probably inevitable.

Being thus stratified, Protestant churches are also quite likely to be class-conscious. A major Protestant denomination which, in the years after World War II, had a very successful program of visitation evangelism, gathered comments from church members on what had happened in their churches. One comment was, "Dr. 'Jones' is ruining our church with the kind of people he's bringing into it." A class distribution of this familiar sort may be inevitable. It is not inevitable, but deplorable, that churches should be class-conscious.

For Protestantism, and for Christianity as a whole, this situation has a history. The Christians of the first century with some exceptions belonged to the poorer classes of society. It was probably widely true, as Paul wrote to the Corinthians, that "not many of you were wise according to worldly standards, not many were powerful, not many were of noble birth" (I Cor. 1:26). Being relatively unhampered by social status or worldly possessions, the earliest Christians were free to accept the Christian gospel wholeheartedly and without compromise. As time went on, this situation changed, and Christianity moved from the spiritual freedom of a poor and persecuted minority to the restrictions of state recognition in the late Roman Empire, and then to the religiosocial amalgamation of all institutions in a medieval society that was "Christian" in theological perspective, but very unchristian in its social stratification and brutal injustice.

The Reformation truly reformed the church, and did much to restore a simple and rigorous New Testament faith. But it also put the Protestant churches into a new relationship of subservience to secular power and influence. Luther, a man of great courage and faith, yet lacked the courage and faith to make the churches truly free. Appalled by the Peasants' Revolt and the excesses of the sectarians, he accepted a relationship of church to state that has continued to afflict the church in all Lutheran countries.

Kierkegaard saw this and commented on it tartly: "Luther really did incalculable harm by not becoming a martyr" (*Journals*, p. 497). Kierkegaard rather deliberately selected the Lutheran identification of church with state as the real villain, the archenemy of Christianity. But in his day and ours (as indeed S. K. knew), much of the mediocrity of Christians and the perversion of Christianity that he attributes to the Establishment can be traced to causes that are both more subtle and more widely prevalent.

When Luther freed the churches that became Protestant from the control of an ecclesiastical hierarchy, he deliberately made them more subject to state control. But this was not all; he also made them more subject to the controls of social tradition and prejudice. The religion of American Protestants has become an astonishing congery of mores and folkways bearing only a faint resemblance to the Christianity of the New Testament. Yet remote though it may be from Christianity, every congregation holds to its close-knit structure of semipagan beliefs and prejudices with genuine earnestness and with only a limited tolerance of deviationists, even though by New Testament standards the deviation might be genuinely Christian.

There is in our day a widespread Biblical and theological enlightenment that gives promise of being a potential corrective of this American pseudo-Christianity. But up to now the light that sometimes is visible in theological discussions in seminaries and conferences, or in courageous pronouncements of church bodies, has achieved no real penetration of this folk religion at the congregational level. No Protestant denomination has overhead organization or leadership that can control or redirect it. A minister trespasses upon its sacrosanctities at his own peril. Currently these sacrosanctities include ideas of racial superiority (not just in the South, but almost everywhere), the exclusive rightness of capitalism (and the wickedness of socialism), the ecclesiastical infallibility of the local Lowells and Cabots, and the holiness and inviolability of everything established by custom and tradition (or, in suburbia, of everything new and different).

The particular sanctities of local congregations will vary widely, though there is also much that is common to the "American way of life" which makes them similar in their general assumptions and loyalties. The gospel of Christ has no more chance of being effectively proclaimed to American congregations in our day than it did in Denmark in 1855. Ministers are, by and large, caught in the same trap of needing to "succeed" as were the priests of the Danish Lutheran Church. Americans want their ministers to be like themselves rather than men of God. We are a generation of organization men and suburbanite women—social conformists to whom the radical character of the Christian faith is an offense and a stumbling block.

The pastor of almost any American congregation, urban or rural, is under tremendous pressure to conform. He may wistfully wish to serve God; he *must* serve his congregation. In numerous ways he can with impunity fail to do the former; if he fails to do the latter, his failure is conspicuous and may be catastrophic for his career.

The principal objection to the union of Christianity and the state in an established church is conflict of interest. In such a situation, a minister's income and professional advancement depend upon his obedience and loyalty to a secular power. Christianity requires his obedience to God above all other considerations. The two are bound to conflict. It is this conflict which Kierkegaard recognized and denounced.

However, in a country where separation of church and state has prevailed throughout our national history, ministers are still confronted by a conflict of interest. The pressures of a secular society are not escaped by avoiding the legal entanglements of "establishment." Society needs religion, but seeks always to shape religion to its own ends. Into Christianity, American society has subtly introduced its own idolatries; and, not so subtly, continues to disregard the prophetic elements of Biblical faith—those elements which would upset the *status quo* and disturb the complacencies of "Christians." Its easy identification of Christianity with folk religion is the demonic confusion of American Protestantism in our time.

The attitudes of Protestant ministers toward this situation classify them in three groups. There is one group—perhaps a growing one—who are aware of the situation and disturbed by it. There is a second group who are so immersed in the traditional and routine pursuits of the ministry and so lost in the culture patterns of our society that they are unaware of any conflict. These are sincere but stupid men. There is a third group composed of ministers who are aware of the conflict between the lives they live and the gospel they should proclaim, but are cynical about it. They have no real commitment to

Christ, but they are competent actors. They have a "good racket" in the ministry, and exploit it for all it is worth. These malodorous characters smell to high heaven, and they have no fear of hell because they do not really believe that there is a hell—or a heaven.

Quite as serious as the problem of discovering a worthy, dedicated, and courageous ministry is the problem of a laity immersed in folk religion. This was Kierkegaard's real concern. He recognized that, for most laymen, "everything is all right" in the brand of Christianity put before them by their ministers. Here we have the paradox that the layman is both the victim who desperately needs the gospel, and confidingly accepts what is preached to him as the true gospel when it is not, and the villain who is responsible for the whole situation because he tacitly demands a watered-down Christianity. For S. K.'s "plain Christian," i.e., the ordinary layman, is virtually helpless to distinguish between the true and the spurious in the messages proclaimed to him in all earnestness from the pulpit. S. K. issues this warning:

> It is a path full of dangers along which thou goest toward the reckoning of eternity. . . . Therefore wake up, be on thy guard, lest thou mightest think to secure eternity for thyself by taking part in what is only a new sin. (*Attack*, p. 60.)

Laymen today are largely unwarned of the specious and spurious "Christianity" that is accepted for the real thing in many churches and by Americans in general. Every man has the right to have the gospel proclaimed and made clear to him. It is the responsibility of the church and of its ministers to confront men with the claim of Christ upon their lives in all its stark intransigence. It is every man's privilege, then, to choose to accept or reject that claim. It must also be made clear to him that, with that choice, he accepts the consequences, now and eternally.

CHAPTER THREE

Statistical Christianity

IT HAS BEEN many years now since I heard a seminary president confess to the senior class of which I was a member that it was virtually impossible for him to know with any accuracy what most of the alumni were really achieving in their pastorates. Yet he was often asked by an alumnus to present his name to a "vacant" church. If the church the alumnus had served was a small one, the president's standard procedure was to turn to the annual reports of the denomination and check on the statistical record of the particular church in the years during which this alumnus had been its pastor. If the report indicated that there had been at least one addition to the membership on confession of faith in Christ for each year, the president would conclude that the man was working with some faithfulness at what ought to be his main job, and would write the requested recommendation.

This anecdote could serve as a parable of what is happening to the church in our time. Our country is large in population and growing rapidly larger. Our major denominations are large and growing larger. The efficient and obvious way to measure the results of our efforts is through annual reports which, in the nature of the case, are largely statistical. So familiar have we become with this means of measuring the progress of the Kingdom of God that we take it for granted that it is a valid indicator. Indeed we take it quite seriously, and the minister whose church does not show statistical increases in membership and budget in successive annual reports is regarded by denominational administrators as a man who "doesn't do anything."

Kierkegaard would surely point out to us that we are laboring under the delusion of numbers. Just as the Danes arrived at the idea that theirs was a Christian nation "by adding up units which are not Christian" (*Attack*, p. 31), so American churches are arriving at their currently impressive statistical totals by counting members, many of whom are not Christians in any proper sense of that word.

Every denomination with a sizable membership (except the Church of Christ, Scientist) publishes an annual report. These reports typically include the actions of governing bodies, activities of denominational agencies, financial summaries, and column after column of names of churches and ministers with associated statistics of membership, accessions and losses, monies raised for various purposes, etc. From time to time some worthy agency of the denomination will succeed in adding a column or symbol that will represent a measurement of denominational performance in the area of its particular concern. Year after year it is the tendency for such reports to proliferate and for the volumes containing them to become thicker and thicker.

The National Council of Churches brings together a summary of this information from all the churches in its annual volume, *Yearbook of American Churches*. From the 1962 edition of this publication, for an example, we glean the following information:

The 259 religious bodies reporting claimed a total membership of 114,449,217. The total number of clergy was 371,258, of whom 241,268 were pastors of churches.

There were 318,697 local churches. If, for our purposes, we exclude Buddhist and Jewish statistics, the religious bodies claiming to be in some way Christian reported a membership of slightly over 109 million, with some 314,-000 churches, 238,000 pastors, and an approximate total of 367,000 clergy. (*Yearbook of American Churches 1962: Information on All Faiths in the U.S.A.*, ed. by Benson Y. Landis, p. 248.)

Because of the time lag in the gathering of reports and the processes of publication, most of these statistics actually represent in part the calendar year 1960 and in part the calendar year 1959. Some statistics also represent the calendar year 1958, but the *Yearbook* carefully specifies these instances.

The total membership of religious bodies reporting represented 63.6 percent of the 1960 population of the United States. Church membership in this country has for many years increased more rapidly than the general population. The comparable 1959 figure was 63.4 percent, and in the year before that, church membership was an even 63 percent of the total population. In the most recent report there had been a membership gain in the churches of 1.9 percent, while the population of the United States had increased 1.8 percent in the same period. (*Ibid.*, pp. 247–248.)

This upward trend in the percentage of Americans who are church members has been reasonably continuous for more than a century, and is a remarkable social phenomenon. In 1850 only 16 percent of the American people were church members. By 1900 this figure had increased to 36 percent. In 1910 and 1920 it was 43 percent; in 1930, 47 percent; in 1940, 49 percent, and in 1950, 57 percent. (*Ibid.*, p. 274.)

Attendance at church services and Sunday school enrollment have also increased in recent years, though not at such a remarkable rate as has church membership. In fact, both church attendance and Sunday school enrollment reached a peak in 1955 and 1956, and have tended to level off since. (*Ibid.*, pp. 276–278.)

We may note that financially the churches are "in the money." For the calendar year 1958, 49 Protestant and Eastern Orthodox bodies reported total contributions of $2,407,464,641. Only 35 of these denominations had reported comparable figures in the previous year. These 35 reported that contributions had increased 6.6 percent over the calendar year 1957. Per capita giving had also increased in these groups from $66.10 per member in 1957 to $69.13 per member in 1958. (*Ibid.*, p. 271.)

Figures quoted from the United States Department of Commerce in the *Yearbook* indicate a vast increase in expenditures for new church buildings. In 1930, according to the Department of Commerce estimate, American churches spent $135 million for new buildings. By 1940, at the end of the depression, church building expenditures had dwindled to $59 million. The churches have taken their full share of the post World War II building boom. By 1950, the amount spent for new church buildings had zoomed to $409 million, and by 1960 to $1,016,-000,000. (*Ibid.*, p. 279.)

If willingness to give is a measure of the willingness of American Christians to sacrifice, it would appear on the surface that there is an unsuspected dimension of depth here. We must not assume this too hastily, however. Figures on per capita giving that are exactly comparable to those we have cited were not available to the writer. The following statistics, however, are of interest in this connection:

According to the 1960 U.S. Statistical Abstract, gifts in this country for religion and welfare rose from an average of $5.00 per capita per year from 1909 to 1914 to $23.00 in 1958. Even when adjustment is made for devaluations of the dollar, Americans are now giving more than did our predecessors. *But* in 1909 the per capita giving amounted to 1.7 percent of what was available to give, and in recent years, it has ranged from 1.3 percent to as low as 1.1 percent of our disposable dollar. With all the channels open to us for giving today, we sacrifice less than did our predecessors. (*The Chicago Theological Seminary Register,* Vol. LII, No. 3, March 31, 1962, p. 8.)

Although his church contributions are not all that a Protestant gives—he contributes to many other causes—it is to be doubted that giving $69.12 to his church represents real sacrifice. His expenditures for all purposes were probably not less than those of the average American, and in 1958 the average American spent $1,097. (See tables in *Information Please Almanac 1960,* ed. by Dan Golenpaul, p. 556; McGraw-Hill Book Company, Inc., 1959.) This figure does not include taxes, which are not exactly voluntary expenditures. It does include giving. The Protestant's gift to his church of $69.12 represents a little more than 6 percent of his spending, commendable perhaps, but hardly sacrificial. When one considers that savings are excluded from these calculations supplied by the U.S. Department of Commerce, American Protestants could hardly (and with a straight face) say with Peter, "Lo, we have left all, and followed thee" (Luke 18:28, KJV).

To return to our main point, however, American Protestantism has certainly become statistically minded. We are also money-minded and building-minded. There is nothing wrong with statistics as such, but can they measure what we as Christians are trying to be and do? There is nothing wrong with money or with having money or giving money, but are we using it as a palliative or a covering mechanism for the emptiness of our souls? There is nothing wrong with buildings as such, but have they become for us a source of pride, a status symbol, a specious species of idolatry? Do we think that all this is Christianity? Or that it is evidence of *our* Christianity? Have we made means into ends so impressively that we have lost sight of the true goals of Christian faith?

STATISTICAL MADNESS

Kierkegaard regarded numbers as antithetical to Christianity. An essay in *The Instant*, of July 7, 1855, was titled "True Christians/Many Christians." He points out that as soon as our measure of Christianity is numbers the goal becomes one of getting as many "Christians" as possible.

> And that's very easily done, it's nothing at all: let's get hold of the children, then each child is given a drop of water on the head—then he is a Christian. If a portion of them don't even get their drop, it comes to the same thing, if only they imagine they got it, and imagine consequently that they are Christians. So in a very short time we have more Christians than there are herring in the herring season, Christians by the millions. (*Attack*, p. 147.)

Could our typically American balloon of statistical Christianity be punctured with neater satire? Statistics, indeed, have no relevance to Christianity. Church members can be counted; Christians can't. No one knows how many Christians there are in America, nor can anyone ever know. Yet we continue, as did the Danes of Kierkegaard's day, under the illusion of numbers. From the aphorism that a Christian is willing to "stand up and be counted" we leap to the conclusion that all who happen to be standing up are Christians!

In the perspective of the New Testament, the idea that a nation could be all Christian (e.g., Denmark in the nineteenth century) or two-thirds Christian (the United States now) is patently absurd. The early Christians were clearly aware of the antithesis between church and world. One can be a Christian only as he is willing to be different from the citizens of this world. Kierkegaard put it this way:

> Christianity is inversely proportionate to number; for the concept "Christian" is a polemical concept, one can only be a Christian in contrast or contrastedly. So it is also in the New Testament: to God's desire to be loved, which is essentially a relationship of contrast, . . . corresponds the fact that the Christian who loves God in contrast and opposition to other men has to suffer from their hate and persecution. (*Ibid.*, p. 127.)

S. K. put this quite bleakly! Many will disagree with what they regard as an unjustifiably extreme statement. Discount Kierkegaard if you will, but do not dismiss him lightly. In the perspective of New Testament Christianity, what he says is essentially true. Christianity, as we have said and will say again, is a demanding faith. No one can love God and not hate evil. It is required of the Christian that he hate the evil in the world, and there is much of it.

Evil can be philosophically explained as being somehow necessary to the good, but it is still to be recognized for what it is—the antithesis and enemy of the good.

The evils of the world, i.e., society, are moral evils, evils resulting from human sin. It is a Christian's vocation in the world to express the love of God in his heart in two visible ways. One is loving service to his fellowmen; the other is the purity of his own life before men. This is quaintly expressed in the language of the King James Version: "to visit the fatherless and widows in their affliction, and to keep himself unspotted from the world" (James 1:27).

It is the fashion of our time to be quite urgent about the first—kindness to the unfortunate, social service— but to disregard the second. This generation of church members, as we have seen, is a conformist generation. The society of which we are a part sets little premium on moral integrity, and neither do church members. The most successful embezzler in recent years was an active churchwoman and a liberal giver to many worthy causes. One of the most colossal frauds in the financial history of our country has recently been perpetrated by a man said to have been a very faithful churchman who participated in many activities of his church, including prayer meetings! These are not isolated examples. Dishonesty and the sins of the flesh are almost as common among church members as they are in the general population. Sins of the spirit, such as pride and envy, are perhaps even more common.

It seems clear that we in the church are not notably unspotted. We have conformed to the world; and much of our immorality is a protective coloration. We do not want to be too different from the citizens of this world. The moral confusion, the immoral complacency, and the generous sinning of our time have so widely infected the membership of our churches that while membership is at an all-time high, so are crime, divorce, suicide, and juvenile delinquency. Our zeal for numbers has made church membership mean almost nothing. Many are delinquents rather than disciples, but we count them all, 109 million members!

The dishonesty of statistical Christianity is a collective sin for which we must all share the blame. However, it would compound the dishonesty not to point out that denominational leaders have a vested interest in this situation. Pastors of large churches, bishops, district superintendents, synod executives, presidents, board secretaries—under whatever name they render their disservice to God—would be hard put to it to retain their jobs or justify their occupational existence if they could gather no "encouraging" statistics and make no impressive reports. Their very presence in the Protestant picture and their proliferation in numbers year by year are posited upon the delusion that a "big operation" is evidence of the growth of the Kingdom of God. Stupendous!

In a contribution to the Copenhagen paper *The Fatherland*, on March 26, 1855, Kierkegaard wrote these pungent words:

> We have, if you will, a complete crew of bishops, deans, and priests; learned men, . . . talented, gifted, humanly well-meaning; they all declaim—doing it well, very well, eminently well, or tolerably well or badly— but not one of them is in the character of the Christianity of the New Testament. But if such is the case, the existence of this Christian crew is so far from being, Christianly considered, advantageous to Christianity that it is far rather a peril, because it is so infinitely likely to give rise to a false impression and the false inference that when we have such a complete crew we must of course have Christianity too. (*Ibid.*, p. 29.)

An added danger of this numbers game in which American Protestantism is merrily engaged is that even earnest Christians will be lulled into complacency by the big numbers. It is clear in Biblical faith that numbers are not to be relied upon as a source of strength. This was an important item of faith with even the earliest prophets. Consider, if you will, the story of the taking of a military census by King David in II Sam., ch. 24. David, trusting in numbers and military might—his own power rather than the power of God—has Joab take a census of males of military age from Dan to the Negeb. Joab protests the order, and David's conscience is uneasy, but he insists that the census be taken. After it is completed, with what should have been reassuring results (1,300,000 valiant men!), David's guilty conscience overwhelms him. He repents and seeks God's forgiveness in prayer. The prophet Gad brings the king God's answer: David and the whole nation are under judgment, and David may choose whichever he regards as the least of three punishments. The king chooses a three-day pestilence in which 70,000 Hebrews die. Jerusalem, however, is not immediately affected, for God in his mercy stays the hand of the angel of death at the threshing floor of Araunah, the Jebusite.

In agony of spirit for the innocent people who have suffered for his sin, David prays that Jerusalem may be spared. At this juncture Gad again brings God's message. David is to erect an altar to the Lord on the threshing floor of Araunah. So, after some dickering with Araunah (who wants to give him the property), the king purchases the threshing floor for fifty silver shekels. The altar having been built, peace offerings and burnt offerings are earnestly made, and the plague is ended. The threshing floor of Araunah was to become, in the providence of God, the site of the Hebrew Temple.

Here we have a story of human pride—statistical arrogance, if this is not stretching the point—and of punishment in which, as so often happens, the innocent suffer for the guilty. It is also a story of human repentance and divine mercy and forgiveness. If we believe, as some of us earnestly do, that the church is the new Israel of God, a chosen people, then we also must repent our idolization of numbers, and trust in his power alone, or our hope is vain.

Insofar as our large (and padded) memberships are a source of pride or of false confidence, we become idolatrous. Burgeoning memberships and impressive statistical reports may fairly be regarded as among the baalim of our time. It is, speaking humbly, a temptation similar to that presented to our Lord when Satan showed him the kingdoms of the world and the glory of them. If we are truly to seek first the Kingdom of God, we must reject all reliance on the empty successes that statistics can measure. There is no assurance and no safety in numbers.

"Godly" Materialism

Christianity is not abstractly spiritual. It has a realistic view of the the world and of human nature. It does not (except for heresies like Christian Science) deny the existence of matter. Nor does it regard matter as evil, and set up a dichotomy of spirit and matter. Man is body and spirit, a whole man. The whole man sins, and the whole man is redeemed by the blood of Christ in his sacrificial death.

The material universe and all things in it have been

created by God, and all things are, in themselves, good. Only when man misuses things do they become evil because they are used to serve evil purposes.

When we have said all this, however, we must assert with Kierkegaard that man is uniquely spirit in contradistinction to all God's other creatures. The Christian is a spiritual man, for God is a Spirit, and one who would know, love, and obey him must be spirit also. The spiritual for Kierkegaard is not mysticism. Mysticism, he suspected, leads one to pantheism, the false identification of self and God.

True spirituality is individual, an experience of aloneness. Only as an individual stands alone before God does he come to know God and know the truth. This is what S. K. meant when he said that truth is subjectivity; truth can be real only to the individual. If it is not known to an individual, it is not known, and it is not truth.

Spirituality is apprehension of spiritual truth. It is impossible to the crowd, or to the man who has no self-awareness apart from his membership in the crowd, who lives always gregariously, who cannot stand to be alone. To have any comprehension of the truth that makes men free, spiritual truth, one must have the courage to be an individual, able and willing to be alone. The movement of an individual toward God is a movement away from the crowd, from earthly reward or honors, from public life in all its forms, from neat systems of thought, from speculative philosophy—away from all these to the simple and personal. For only the individual exists for that individual himself; and only the individual can attain that purity of heart which is to will one thing: to live obediently before God.

It is in aloneness that an individual knows both his own sinfulness and, paradoxically, his own preciousness to God. It is in aloneness that he experiences God's forgiveness, and discovers his true vocation as a Christian. None of this can happen to the person who is never alone, who has no aloneness, who loses himself in "togetherness." " 'The individual' is the category of the spirit," says Kierkegaard, and "of spiritual awakening." (*Point of View*, p. 132.)

Protestantism in America in the mid-twentieth century does not cultivate individuality. Its effort is to bring people together in groups, and its zeal is for large groups, perhaps for worship, perhaps for study and discussion, perhaps for sheer sociability. We hear much about "group dynamics." People are to be pulled together into a sort of "suburbanite" togetherness. In fact, the largest member denomination in the National Council of Churches publishes a magazine for adults entitled *Together*. (I do not presume to comment on this; I merely mention it. But I think I would enjoy S. K.'s comment if only we could have it!)

All our denominations bring people together for services of "public worship." The public character of these "services" (we are not clear whom they serve) does not make it impossible for an individual to experience the presence of God, but varying degrees of both formality and folksiness make them deadening or distracting as the case may be, and one may fairly doubt if much worship actually takes place.

This is no diatribe against corporate worship (the Holy Spirit was given at Pentecost in what seems to have been an assemblage for corporate worship). Nor should we impugn the earnestness of many ministers and many lay worshipers. They are trying, and many do really worship. There are, however, many handicaps. To attend "church" is a habit with many people, and with some it is a mere habit to go, just as it is the habit of others to stay away. It doesn't mean too much to either group. This is why it is so easy for people who have attended church services regularly to drop the habit entirely when they move to another community. It is also the case in many places that surburbia has invaded the sanctuary, and people go to church for quite other reasons than to worship. Some, of course, go to church because it is a *good* thing to do, not because they expect or experience any real encounter with God. Still less hopefully, there are some in church because it is *the* thing to do.

It would be a rash generalization to say that the motivation for the wave of interest in religion and the high level of church attendance in recent years has been due entirely to conformity. Herberg, Eckardt, Berger, and others have discussed this, and have carefully explored the possible causes. (See Will Herberg, *op. cit.*; A. Roy Eckardt, *The Surge of Piety in America,* Association Press, 1958; Peter L. Berger, *The Precarious Vision,* Doubleday & Company, Inc., 1961.) The causes, however, seem to be largely psychological and sociological; there is a widespread need for psychological aid and comfort (a tranquilizer) and for social support and fulfillment. Even patriotism is a factor, as in the American Legion's "Back to God" movement. By aligning oneself with the church, one lines up against godless communism.

It is not my purpose to pass judgment on these motives. They are prudential, and perhaps proper, in a context of secular, socially oriented morality. But the religion that results is not Christianity. It is a religion that can and does appraise itself in terms of externals—larger congregations, numerous church-sponsored organizations and activities, beautiful and efficient buildings, bigger and bigger budgets. The church building boom is symbolic of the best and the worst in Protestantism. It is potentially a genuine expression of Christian stewardship when people give generously in order that the worship and educational activities of the churches may be adequately housed and equipped. But it is far from Christian to take pride in these externals, or to regard them as ends instead of means and therefore measures of the advancement of God's Kingdom.

Americans *are* materialistic! They measure the worth of everything in quantitative terms. Children and young people are taught this even in our "character-building" programs: Boy Scouts learn citizenship or craft skills or wildlife only incidentally; what they really learn is to accumulate merit badges. Hollywood has taught us to judge by appearance, and if we have any more solid basis of measuring a man's worth, it is by his bank account. So it is no wonder that even when Americans are interested in their churches, their interest expresses itself in bigger and more beautiful buildings. Between 1946 and 1960, Americans spent $7,300,000,000 for new church construction, and the rate of recent construction has been one new church every eight hours. (See Claire Cox, *op. cit.*, p. 154.)

In present thinking about the responsibility of the church, some part of this vast expenditure is for necessary construction. Churches must be built where people are, and Americans are moving. But there is also much extravagance, competitiveness, and false pride. There is an element of Christian zeal here, and some of the giving is sacrificial. When we have said this, however, we must also be reminded that Christianity was founded by a Galilean peasant. He never laid a cornerstone or dedicated a new building. He did most of his preaching out of doors, and exerted his most profound influence through intensive work with a small group. He pronounced a damning judgment upon the only outstanding religious edifice of his nation and time, and accurately predicted its destruction. He owned only the clothes he wore, and, at the end, these were taken from him down to the simplest undergarment, and he had left only a cross.

There were no buildings belonging to early Christianity. Paul was a busy bishop, but there is no record that he ever broke ground for a new church edifice in Antioch, Corinth, Ephesus, or anywhere else. When he was driven from the synagogues, he "hired a hall," or preached in homes, or out of doors. To him the church was the body of Christ, a fellowship of the saints. To the writer of the letter to the Hebrews it was an "assembly of the first-born." It was never, for the early Christians, a building.

Church buildings are an inheritance from the Jewish synagogue and the pagan temples. Would the church be truer to its Lord if it had no buildings, if what we call a church were a little group of earnest believers meeting in a home, if there were no budgets and no paid ministry? It is, I realize, fantastic to raise such questions. They are, however, worth meditating upon, and such meditations might reorient us helpfully to the whole vast organizational machinery, feverish activities, and material equipment of American churches. Kierkegaard's comment was this:

> We have what one might call a complete inventory of churches, bells, organs, benches, alms boxes, foot warmers, tables, hearses, etc. But when Christianity does not exist, the existence of this inventory, so far from being, Christianly considered, an advantage, is far

rather a peril, because it is so infinitely likely to give rise to a false impression and the false inference that when we have such a complete Christian inventory we must of course have Christianity too. (*Attack*, p. 30.)

Our statistics are meaningless, and our buildings are sepulchers of a dead faith, unless there are also individuals who know God, who live in grateful, humble, self-denying faith, and in whose hearts there is a love of God and of fellowmen that moves them to seek first God's Kingdom. Without the existential faith of individuals, our reports are empty bombast, and our sanctuaries with their symbols of worship are mere things. Indeed they are idolatrous because we make them ends in themselves, false ultimates of a faith that has been short-circuited and yields us no real power. Like all idols, they deceive not only the sophisticated who should know better, but also (and tragically) the innocent and the unwary, the plain men and women who think *this* is Christianity.

Consider, if you will, two recommendations, both of which are Kierkegaardian in mood:

1. Declare a ten-year moratorium on statistics. Let us have reports, but put them in the form of case histories or human-interest stories of anonymous but real individuals to whom the saving gospel of Christ has come with new power. Include, if desired, some description of means and methods by which men have been confronted with Christ and brought into the circle of God's grace, but—no statistics!

2. For ten years build no new church buildings except those obviously and desperately needed in unchurched areas. Make those which are built simple structures, prefabricated perhaps, but inexpensive, unpretentious, functional.

These recommendations will, of course, not be accepted or followed. They will not even be considered, for they are quite unacceptable to a church bound by pagan traditions, infiltrated by secular culture, and dazed by its own bedazzlements.

CHAPTER FOUR

Ministers Are Hypocrites

DURING the long period of silence that preceded Kierkegaard's attack on Christendom, he wrote much in his *Journals*. He was accumulating material in preparation for the attack. When the attack came, he used very little of this material. Dr. Walter Lowrie quite properly included some of it in his English translation of the work now entitled *Attack Upon "Christendom."* Here is a relevant sample.

> When I think of what in my father's time was understood by shop clerk: an awkward Jewish bumpkin—and of what now is understood by it: a nimble, brisk fellow, . . . this indeed is progress of a sort.
>
> It is pretty much the same now with a modern clergyman: a nimble, adroit, lively man, who in pretty language, with the utmost ease, with graceful manners, etc., knows how to introduce a little Christianity, but as easily . . . as possible. In the New Testament, Christianity is the profoundest wound that can be inflicted upon a man, calculated on the most dreadful scale to collide with everything—and now the clergyman has perfected himself in introducing Christianity in such a way that it signifies nothing, and when he is able to do this to perfection he is regarded as a paragon. (P. 258.)

Even more satirical is the following passage, originally published in *The Instant* of August 30, 1855. S. K. quotes Matt. 4:19, "Follow me, and I will make you fishers of men," and comments that to the original apostles this meant sacrifice. He continues:

> What Christ meant is something quite different from what these honest apostles achieved, in defiance of all linguistic usage and linguistic analogy, for in no language is this what is understood by fishing. What he meant and intended was the origination of a new branch of business, i.e., man fishery, preaching Christianity in such a way that it will amount to something to fish with this fishing company. . . .
>
> It was quite simply arranged. Just as one company is formed to speculate in the herring-fishery, another in cod-fishing, another in whaling, etc., so man-fishing was carried on by a stock company which guaranteed its members a dividend of such and such a percent.
>
> And what was the result of it? . . . The result was that they caught a prodigious number of herring, or what I mean is men, Christians; and of course the company was in a brilliant financial condition. It proved indeed that even the most successful herring company did not make nearly so big a profit as did man-fishery. And one thing further, an extra profit, or at least a piquant seasoning on top of the profit, namely, that no herring company is able to quote words of Scripture when they send boats out for the catch.
>
> But man-fishery is a godly enterprise; the stockholders in this company can appeal to words of Scripture for themselves, for Christ says, "I will make you fishers of men." They can tranquilly go to meet the Judgment, saying, "We have accomplished thy word, we have fished for men." (*Attack*, pp. 203–204.)

Seldom has the Christian ministry been subjected to more scathing sarcasm, even from its avowed enemies. If now we become objective for the moment (a very un-Kierkegaardian approach), and analyze the criticisms leveled at the priests of the Danish Lutheran Church by S. K., they can be roughly summarized as follows.

1. Men enter the ministry with self-seeking motives—motives that are far removed from seeking first the Kingdom of God.

2. There is little real sacrifice involved in the life of the average minister; but the gospel he is required to proclaim is one of sacrifice and voluntary suffering. He makes a good living by preaching a gospel he doesn't practice.

3. A wife is an insidious sort of handicap to a minister's wholehearted dedication to Christ's service.

4. The whole pattern of life in church and society obligates a minister to divided loyalties, and makes it virtually impossible for him to find any honorable escape from the patent hypocrisies of his situation.

A Young Man's Motives

Kierkegaard's example of the typical ministerial candidate is his "Ludwig From." Ludwig, says S. K., is "seeking." One would naturally suppose that it is the Kingdom of God which he seeks. But not so! Ludwig is nearing the completion of his theological preparation for the Lutheran priesthood. "What he seeks is a royal appointment to a living." (*Ibid.*, p. 208.) After eleven years of arduous study (high school, college, seminary), he feels himself entitled to a pastorate. Indeed the last two and a half years of his seminary course have been spent "seeking."

> His life, which hitherto cannot be said to have had any relation to the absolute, suddenly assumes such a relation: he seeks absolutely everything; he writes one sheet after another of officially stamped paper, filling four pages of each; he runs from Herod to Pilate; he recommends himself to the ministers of state and to the

porters; in short he is entirely in the service of the absolute. (*Ibid.*, p. 208.)

After such superhuman efforts in the pursuit of very human ends, Ludwig receives his appointment. Then he discovers that this "living" provides about $150 less than he had expected. He is in despair! He is on the point of rejecting the "call" when an acquaintance persuades him to accept it anyway. So, in due course, he is ordained and installed.

The Dean, who presents Ludwig to the congregation, has, like all priests, "an unprejudiced eye for earthly profit," and knows that Ludwig has almost rejected the appointment for the want of the $150. "By a stroke of genius," the Dean chooses as his text: "Lo, we have left all, and followed thee." Ludwig follows, basing his sermon on the gospel for the day, which is (what a coincidence!): "Seek ye first the kingdom of God." The young man does very well and is commended by the Bishop, who is also present, for his effort, especially for his emphasis upon *first* in "Seek ye first the kingdom."

The story is a deftly drawn comedy of human blindness and fatuity. It is a comedy that is being reenacted over and over again in contemporary American Protestantism. Humorously viewed, it is just as funny now as it was in Denmark in Kierkegaard's day. But it is a comedy with tragic implications. Young men are entering the ministry with mixed motives. Some of these motives may be Christian, but prominent also are the goals of success common to our secular culture. There is widespread confusion about the function of the ministry among ministers and particularly in Protestant theological seminaries. The recent study of theological education directed by the late H. Richard Niebuhr, Daniel Day Williams, and James M. Gustafson has revealed some aspects of this confusion. The seminaries are characterized by denominational provincialism, ecclesiasticism, Biblicism, and "Christism," and by many other "less deceptive, cruder substitutions of the proximate for the ultimate" (*The Purpose of the Church and Its Ministry*, p. 46; Harper & Row, Publishers, Inc., 1956).

Those confusions mentioned are the more respectable idolatries of current theological education. Unmentioned, for instance, is the sheer professionalism that dominates the atmosphere of the theological schools, emphasizing exegetical, homiletical, and administrative skills, and ministerial success in these matters at the expense of commitment and evangelical zeal.

The report concludes: "Our schools, like our churches and our ministers, have no clear conception of what they are doing, but are carrying on traditional actions, making separate responses to various pressures exerted by churches and society, contriving uneasy compromises among many values, engaging in little quarrels symptomatic of undefined issues, trying to improve their work by adjusting minor parts of the academic machine or by changing the specifications of the raw material to be treated." (*Ibid.*, p. 101.) When the leaders of theological education do not know what they are doing, clarity of purpose and purity of motive are scarcely to be expected of their students. So it was with Ludwig From, and so it is with his American counterpart today.

Students in the current seminary generation are themselves quite critical of the churches and of the educational process to which they are being subjected in seminaries. This has its dangers, but it is also hopeful. They are "seeking," and not just for an attractive "call," though there is still a marked hiatus between their verbalizing and their practice. In practice, when they have completed their theological education, the vast majority of them still seek high salaries, comfortable living conditions, and a wide range of fringe benefits. And the salary differential now is more than a paltry $150 per annum.

Theological schools are not responsible for the kind of candidate material that the church recruits and turns over to them. The problems of vocational and pretheological counseling are perplexing. With the relative immaturity of a college student's own spiritual life, a counselor is puzzled to know how much to expect in terms of clarity and purity of motives for entering the ministry. From my own experience, I recall one student who was at least very honest about his motives. He had lived across the street from a minister in his hometown, and had observed this minister's daily routine—the easy hours spent on the front porch of the parsonage reading a book, waving to passing motorists, and chatting with pedestrians; the time available for golf; the fun had with youth groups; etc. He was well paid, liked by everyone, had enjoyable work and cradle-to-grave security. Where could anyone find a better deal? So this young man had chosen the ministry.

This is admittedly an extreme case. Most candidates for the ministry are sincere, even if somewhat vague about their purposes. But the difference between this young man and many other aspirants for a ministerial career may be only a matter of a sudden burst of honesty. The real culprit is probably the minister across the street, and there are many "ministers across the street." This is an appropriate point for turning our attention to them.

"Servants of Christ"

It was Kierkegaard's earnest contention that the false form of Christianity which he called Christendom was sustained and perpetuated by the vested interests of the clergy. In the fictitious perspective of Christendom, there were a million people, and therefore a million Christians, in Denmark. The presence of these million Christians required and justified the employment of one thousand priests by the state. Or, says S. K., the argument can be inverted: if there are one thousand priests who make a good living in Denmark, there are obviously a million Christians whose presence and support make these "livings" possible. It is also obvious that in such a situation the priests are pecuniarily interested in having as many people as possible call themselves Christians.

> But nothing is more dangerous to true Christianity . . . than to get men to assume light-mindedly the name of Christian, to teach them to think meanly of what it is to be a Christian, as if it were something one is as a matter of course. And the "priest" is pecuniarily interested in having it stop there, with the assumption of the name Christian, and that men should not learn to know what Christianity truly is. (*Attack*, p. 84.)

Kierkegaard's initial controversy with Bishop Hans Martensen had been over the real qualifications of a "witness to the truth." S. K. suggests that there is a very simple way to discover whether or not the priests are really witnesses to the truth: "Withdraw their whole stipend and save the expense of pensions" (*ibid.*, p. 86).

Our American situation in this seventh decade of the twentieth century is different in numerous and obvious ways. But it is still true that a minister's income and job security depend to a considerable extent on the size of his congregation and his ability to increase it by bringing in new members. New members are received into churches by certificate from other churches or by "profession of faith" without any serious attempt to discover whether or not any of them understands what it means to be a Christian. The minister with the fast-growing church membership (and the fast-growing church budget) is likely to be the man who gets big salary increases or a call to a larger church at a much larger salary.

Strictly from the standpoint of motivation, this situation is not very different from that against which Kierkegaard inveighed. The temptation here is subtle and often irresistible. It is easy for a minister to delude himself into thinking that he is "building the Kingdom of God" when he is really building his own little empire by mass production methods that are completely incompatible with the Christianity of the New Testament. Certainly no one should presume to judge the conscious or unconscious motives of a particular minister; only God can know whether or not he has succumbed to "worldly" motivation. It is remarkable, however, that the call of God to a "larger field of service" almost invariably coincides with a larger salary and greater prestige. This is so common that we take it for granted, and even the jokes we make about it are sorry. We measure a minister's success in these terms, and most ministers accept this as a valid criterion of their own achievement. So firmly entrenched is this standard of measurement that a minister would feel embarrassed, or perhaps disgraced, to accept a call to a smaller church at a lower salary.

Ours is a materialistic civilization. Americans judge quality by the price tag. While denouncing communism as wrong because it proposes an equal distribution of economic goods by ruthless force, we yet accept its basic thesis that man is an economic automaton—a robot incapable of being motivated by any other consideration than his own economic self-interest. The only way to satisfy men is by larger wages or bigger profits. This, of course, is not what we say exactly, but it is the way we operate "when the chips are down."

Ministers must live in this kind of society, a society in which money is the major goal of men's effort and the measure of men's success. It is the responsibility of ministers to live in the world without being conformed to it. But if we may judge by appearances, ministers are not only in the world and of it; they are *for* it!

In the days of my growing up, roughly the first two decades of the century, most ministers received annual salaries of less than $1,000. Manses were by no means so common as now, and there were few, if any, fringe benefits. Salaries and other benefits increased measurably in the twenties, and declined in the depression years of the thirties. The years during and since World War II have seen a determined drive by denominational leaders to increase ministerial salaries, and to improve pension plans and other benefits. It has been the theory that if the Protestant churches are to attract (descriptive word!) able young men into the ministry, they must provide attractive salaries. The mores of our society being what they are, this is probably true. But there is a vast confusion of values here. One should not make sweeping generalizations, of course, about the worldly motives of ministers without noting that most ministers still receive modest salaries and carry on their work with some real sacrifice. There are also big operators in the ministry with big salaries and great prestige. They can still proclaim from the pulpit that Christianity is a demanding faith requiring self-sacrifice and involving suffering. But do they live it? On the contrary, to the best of their financial ability they seem to be living it up!

The ministry has also become a highly competitive occupation. Some years ago it was my privilege to serve and assist one of our larger churches while it was without a pastor. In a denomination which had at that time about nine thousand churches and nine thousand ministers, there were 115 applicants for the pastorate of that church. Some of them applied directly with what I now regard as admirable frankness. Others were more subtle. Whether it was sheer coincidence or the remarkable diligence of the Holy Spirit, as many as eight or ten individuals would be inspired to write almost simultaneously recommending the same minister!

In various forms this ministerial ladder-climbing goes on in all the major Protestant denominations, whether the form of government be episcopal, presbyterian, or congregational. There is little danger that the United States Department of Justice will indict the Protestant ministry for lack of competition. These are the men who, like the priests of the Danish Lutheran Church in Kierkegaard's day, profess to be the servants of Christ. Some of them may have left much to follow him. It can hardly be said that they have left all. If they have a witness, as S. K. pungently remarked, it is "that the never-to-be-forgotten significance of His life is that by His death . . . He made possible a new way of livelihood" (*ibid.,* p. 188).

MARRIAGE: THE TRUE FELICITY

Kierkegaard blamed much of the pecuniary proclivities of Danish Lutheran priests on their concern for family responsibilities. One reason why "Ludwig From" was so disturbed to find that his "living" was $150 less than he had supposed was that he had gotten himself engaged. He must support a wife. S. K. regards marriage as an effective instrument for keeping young men in the ministry and keeping them mediocre. It is by reason of marriage that every clerical appointment must provide a good living.

> A living—and then Juliana, that Frederick and Juliana can come together. . . . If at any moment the thought should struggle in Frederick, "I myself do not really believe this doctrine, and then to have to preach it to others"—if such thoughts should struggle in Frederick, go to Juliana, she can drive such thoughts away. "Sweet Frederick," says she, "only let us manage to come together. Why go and torment thyself with such thoughts? There are surely one thousand priests like thee, in short thou art a priest like the others."
>
> In fact Juliana plays a great role in procuring clergy for the state. And hence they should have been wary about introducing Juliana, and also about introducing livings. For it may be, as Don Juan says to Zerline, that only in the soft arms of a blameless wife does true felicity reside, and possibly it is true, as both poets and prose writers have affirmed, that in these soft arms one forgets the world's alarms; but the question is whether there is not also something else one can only too easily forget in these soft arms—namely, what Christianity is. And the older I grow the clearer it becomes to me that the twaddle into which Christianity has sunk, especially in Protestantism, and more especially in Denmark, is due in part to the fact that these soft arms have come to interfere a little too much, so that for the sake of Christianity one might require the respective proprietors of these soft arms to retire a little more into the background. (*Ibid.*, p. 145.)

Marriage is undoubtedly a deterrent to courageous self-sacrifice on the part of a minister. There is no way in which he can sacrifice himself to witness for the truth without also sacrificing his wife and children. As a married man he is quite properly concerned for the welfare and happiness of his family. He may therefore be led to reject a most challenging call because the manse would be a "woman killer," or the neighborhood in which his family would live is deteriorating, or the local schools are reported to be inferior. Ministers are usually sensitive men and will take such concerns seriously. As a middle-aged woman once said to me, "Ministers make such *sweet* husbands." So they do.

When Luther abandoned the celibacy of the priest-hood, he opened the door to the mediocrity that now characterizes the Protestant ministry. There is much to be said for clerical celibacy. The celibate priest is free to serve and to sacrifice himself in the work of the church, as a married man is not. This is, of course, no guarantee that he will do so. But "the encircling arms" of a loving wife do limit the effectiveness of many a Protestant minister, even when he is a man of deep devotion to Christ.

Wife and family often enable a minister to justify his worldly concern for a larger salary. They close doors for him into fields of service where God could use him most fruitfully if he were celibate. For example, the inner-city church has become, in the past twenty years, a major problem for most Protestant denominations. Such a church has a tremendous opportunity for continuing witness and service among the people who now surround the church building, using its steps for daytime loafing and its stained-glass windows for nocturnal targets. In a thousand such churches today there is need for able ministers who will live among these people, sharing their life and their problems, leading them into the circle of God's grace. But what minister with a family wants to subject his children to these conditions?

In many areas of the world today there is opportunity for the kind of selfless and courageous witness for Christ that a celibate minister can make with greater effectiveness. In the most normal situations married ministers experience the tension between the infinite loyalty that Christ demands and the perfectly proper but finite loyalties of the family relationship. For men who do not feel this compelling loyalty to Christ there is no tension, and for them and their families the ministry becomes merely a livelihood.

There is new life stirring in the Church of Rome. If and as it casts off the hampering weight of its many medievalisms and witnesses to a purer faith, it may be God's chosen vessel. It will have many assets, and not the least of these is a dedicated and celibate priesthood. It may yet be the church of the future, and mediocre Protestantism, which demands little of its leaders or its laity, will be only a name in the history books.

TRIBAL PRESSURES TO CONFORMITY

The pseudodemocratic ideologies that were to eventuate in the totalitarian societies of our time were already strongly advocated in Kierkegaard's day. He was one of the few who saw the danger in them and warned of the results for mankind. It was clear to him that men are not equal in ability, and that the leadership of a society must be in the hands of its best and ablest men, if things are to be well with that society. His emphasis upon the individual was not an irresponsible individualism, for all men are responsible before God. But he had little confidence in the ability of "the public" to rule itself. The vested authorities in both state and church should be men of courage and ability who will form and lead public opinion instead of being merely subservient to it.

S. K. saw the trend of Western society toward leveling and mass conformity, and nothing has happened to stop that trend. Our generation of Americans is a conformist generation. We are tending toward a mass alikeness, not only in clothing, cars, houses, and recreations, but also in our thinking. The society to which Americans conform in our day is highly materialistic, as we have seen. It is the prophetic function of Christian ministers to be nonconformists, to be individuals, both in the inner structure of their motivational life and in their outward and visible habits, attitudes, and relationships. If we may add to David Riesman's well-known categories of tradition-directed, inner-directed, and other-directed types of people (*The Lonely Crowd,* pp. 19–40; Anchor Book, Doubleday & Company, Inc., 1953), a minister, we will say, ought to be God-directed. Riesman, perhaps, would call him inner-directed, a perennially transitional type of character who is never completely at home in the society of which he is a part. To an extent, of course, a minister may be said to be tradition-directed, since his ideological and emotional roots run deeply through the cumulative strata of the past to the first century A.D. Certainly, if he becomes other-directed, one who chooses his views as he chooses his hats—because they are being worn by others—he loses all ability to be a minister of the gospel.

There are such men in the ministry today. As S. K. points out, they are mere tradesmen. When these men become eminent, as some do, they may become popular propagators of the power of positive thinking, or scintillating supersalesmen of a spurious product called peace of soul, or mellifluous merchants of peace of mind. They do not, however, know the mind of Christ. They are so perfectly adjusted to the culture patterns by which, from infancy, they were conditioned, that they know no tensions. Their souls are never a battleground.

This is precisely why Kierkegaard contends that the state can never "protect" Christianity as it professes to do in an established church. The best service the state can render to Christianity, he says, is to persecute it. If this happens, those who remain loyal to Christianity will be Christians at great cost to themselves. They will know what peace means because they have been to the wars. They will understand the peace that Christ gives to those who suffer for him, a peace that passes understanding.

Not that persecution is necessary to the struggles of the soul—if this were true, who could be a Christian in these tolerant times? But unless a minister has known struggle, he has not suffered, he has had no personal need for Christ, and he does not know the depths of Christ's love or the illimitable resources of his power. There must be conflict, or at least tension, and the other-directed man is not likely to experience either one. Many other-directed men get into the ministry. They are usually "nice guys." I once knew one who, ironically, ruined his effectiveness with his congregation because he smiled and smiled at everyone, even at funerals! The other-directed man in the ministry must have what Kierkegaard described as a poet's ability to speak about suffering with apparent conviction, even if there is no reality behind the appearance. This is sometimes described in the jargon of the trade as "tear-jerking," and some have developed such refined techniques for doing this that no one would know that it is a mere technique, behind which, as S. K. would say, is nothing!

Some ministers also become adept at the priestly skill of "applying Christianity tranquilizingly" (*Attack*, p. 262). They give congregations what congregations think they want, and the result is a religion with "the quality of refined hypocrisy" (*ibid.*, p. 201). They may even be able to summon every evidence of deep emotion in the pulpit, but this merely means, as S. K. pointed out, that, in addition to being poets, they are also actors.

The situation of many a minister in a typical middle-class Protestant church is both ludicrous and tragic. I am reminded of the unregenerate character who, when reproved for his profanity by a pious neighbor, replied: "Deacon, I do a little cussin' and you do a little prayin', but neither of us means anything by it." There is a tacit conspiracy between pastor and people—an unexpressed but functioning agreement not to take Christianity too seriously.

The laity, however, while preferring to be deceived, also have the ability to recognize the hypocrisy of a Sunday religion for what it is. One wonders what would be the result for many a well-fed, well-housed, and well-clothed minister if the test which Kierkegaard proposes could be staged in every pulpit across the length and breadth of America. Here it is:

> What I might be tempted to propose is the following order of service: the congregation assembles; a prayer is said at the church door; a hymn is sung; then the priest goes up to the speaker's seat, takes out the New Testament, pronounces the name of God, and thereupon reads from it before the congregation that definite passage, loudly and distinctly, whereupon he has to be silent and to remain standing silently for five minutes in the pulpit, and then he can go. (*Ibid.*, p. 120.)

The passages suggested are Matt. 23:29–33, beginning: "Woe to you, scribes and Pharisees, hypocrites!" and

Luke 11:47–48, beginning: "Woe to you! for you build the tombs of the prophets." I suspect that if this experiment were tried, the results would be disappointing to Kierkegaard. The average American congregation would defend its minister: (1) because they like him; and (2) because they would be more concerned for the impeccability of his public image as *their* minister than for the logical or moral absurdity of his position. Most people simply want their minister to measure up to the standard norms of behavior expected of nice people everywhere. Deviation in the direction of a deeper earnestness and radical action suited to a radical faith will therefore be objected to almost as strenuously as deviation in the opposite direction. People don't want their minister to be either a "fanatic" or a "libertine"; they just want him to be a nice man.

The Protestant minister is cast in one of the most difficult roles imaginable in our society. His role may be compared to that of a tightrope-walking aerial artist in the top of the big tent. His performance is carried on with all eyes upon him. His is primarily a balancing act: he must not fall—he must not even lean—to one side or the other; perfect equilibrium is expected of him at all times. He must also, in the course of his act, perform some brilliant feats of juggling, and he does all this while carrying an unbelievable number of other people on his back.

Like all role-playing, the role of the minister is peculiarly subject to what Jean-Paul Sartre has called "bad faith"; sincerity demands that a man be "for himself only what he is" (*Being and Nothingness*, p. 58; Philosophical Library, Inc., 1956). But it is the human predicament that no one is ever quite what he is. "In this sense," says

Sartre, "it is necessary that we make ourselves what we are." (*Ibid.*, p. 59.) The struggle that each man has with himself and even the idea of sincerity that we hold indicate the gap between what we are and what we must in self-respect fiercely think of ourselves as being. We live always, therefore, as Sartre points out, in bad faith. To be human is to live in bad faith, whether one is conscious of the discrepancy or not. The role of the minister is more difficult than most because he is a human being in a role requiring superhuman abilities and resources.

So long as a man's ideal of his ministry is other-directed, he is conceiving his occupational role at a purely human level, and is in a situation of bad faith bordering on the comic. To the hypocrisy of turning the preaching of self-denial into a neat profit for himself, he adds the deeper one of obeying one master—the public—while professing obedience to another—God. Humanly speaking, there is quite a future in the ministry for the bright young man who can do this well. His is a skill comparable to that of Kierkegaard's hypothetical barber who could "shave off a man's beard without his noticing it" (*Journals,* p. 499). It is a skill that would be admired by pickpockets and prestidigitators.

The other-directed minister, who preaches what men want to hear, is a fraud. His is the most serious of all fraudulent operations because he is defrauding men of their birthright as children of God. Instead of pointing men to the only way that can lead to eternal happiness, he leads them along pleasant paths all of which lead in the opposite direction. Or, to change the figure, in place of the demanding faith of Christianity, he persuades men to accept an adulterated substitute—and this, not because he believes in it, but because it is what people want. What he sells for coffee is not coffee!

There are undoubtedly many inner-directed men in the ministerial leadership of American Protestantism. These men have real tension in all they do—they know "suffering"—because of the conflict of their Christian convictions and insights with the actualities of their situation. Kierkegaard suspected that many Danish Lutheran ministers of his time would have welcomed escape from the ecclesiastical situation that forced continued hypocrisies upon them.

> One becomes a parson at an early age. Then one marries—and has the responsibility of a family. Then doubts arise. But now it is too late, now one must, as we men say, hold one's ears; one is forced farther and farther into untruth, so becomes less and less a Christian, yet more and more defiantly assertive that naturally one is a Christian since one is a teacher in Christendom. (Walter Lowrie, *Kierkegaard,* Vol. II, p. 528; Torchbook, Harper & Row, Publishers, Inc., 1962.)

This is not the whole picture. There must have been many in Denmark, and there must be many in the United States, who were willing to face their situation more honestly and more courageously than this. To be a Christian minister is, spiritually, the most dangerous of all vocations.

> Hence it is a venturesome thing to preach; for when I mount to that sacred place [the pulpit]—whether the church be crowded or as good as empty—I have, though I myself may not be aware of it, one hearer in addition to those that are visible to me, namely, God in heaven,

whom I cannot see, it is true, but who verily can see me. This hearer listens attentively to discover whether what I say is true, and he looks also to discern . . . whether my life expresses what I say. And although I possess no authority to impose an obligation upon any other person, yet what I have said in the course of the sermon puts me under obligation—and God has heard it. Verily, it is a venturesome thing to preach! (*Training in Christianity*, p. 229.)

CHAPTER FIVE

Lay Religion:
"Childishness and Crime"

L AY RELIGION in America—the Christianity of the majority—is still, as it was among the Danes of Kierkegaard's time, "a mixture of childishness and crime" (*Journals*, p. 501). The popular belief, now as then, is that one enters Christianity by becoming as a little child, and then continues in this childish attitude throughout one's adult life. The average Protestant American unites with the church or is confirmed at an age when he has little understanding of what it is all about, and remains in this pristine ignorance the rest of his life. He becomes a spiritual moron, but a shrewd one. Having matured in other ways, all of them typically American, he knows a bargain when he finds one, and God, it seems, is an easy mark. Kierkegaard analyzes it this way:

There is always a worldliness that is desirous of having the name of being a Christian but wishes to become one at as cheap a price as possible. This worldliness took notice of Luther. It listened; it listened carefully again—carefully lest it should have heard wrongly. Thereupon it said, "Excellent! This is something for us. Luther says it depends on faith alone. He himself does not say that his life expresses works, and since he is dead now they are not reality any more. Consequently we take his word, his teaching—and we are free from all works. Long live Luther!" (*For Self-examination*, p. 10.)

Twentieth-century Americans will perhaps be a little more sophisticated about salvation. They really do not like to think about such things at all; they are reminded of dying, and this is a very unpleasant thought. Americans want to think only of pleasant things; and Protestant preaching in American churches has been responsive to popular demand. Even more appropriate to the American scene than it was in nineteenth-century Denmark is Kierkegaard's comment: "Luther, your responsibility is great indeed, for the closer I look the more clearly do I see that you overthrew the pope—and set the public on the throne" (*Journals*, p. 500).

The typical error of Protestant preaching has been to stress human faith and divine grace and neglect human self-discipline and divine judgment. This, of course, has not always and everywhere been true. Puritanism and Victorianism were typical Protestant developments. But the sin of our generation is not the bigoted censoriousness of the caricatured Puritan, nor the shoddy pretense of the much-maligned Victorian. Our sin is the ready identification of what we are with what we ought to be. We want a religion that does not disturb this complacency.

Said Kierkegaard: "It is not possible to regard that as Christianity which men like best and prefer to call Christianity." (*Attack*, p. 32.) The New Testament makes clear what Christianity is. Lay religion in America has little correspondence to it.

Some of the roots of this situation lie in the history of the past century, as has been indicated in Chapter One. In a society that places such emphasis upon the material goods of life, the whole climate of thought has become secularized. "The acids of modernity" have eaten away the reality of the world of the spirit, in which our forefathers firmly believed. The comforts and conveniences of "the good life" that Americans enjoy are obsessive. The luster and marvel of scientific invention and exploration in this age of space have dimmed the certainties of the age of faith. To modern man "the spacious firmament on high" and the "shining frame" of the "spangled heavens" no longer proclaim their great Original. They merely challenge him to continue his probing of outer space, and to get to the moon, if possible, before the Russians do.

So, added to the common tendency of mankind to worldly ease of which Kierkegaard writes, we have now an artless and nearly complete obsession with the affairs of this world. Men come to church now seeking the *values* of religion. Church membership and attendance have become a functional device for meeting human needs. Psychiatrists recommend religion, and juvenile court judges sentence teen-agers to regular attendance at Sunday school. Whatever it is that is to be gained from being religious, this it is that laymen seek—for themselves and for their children.

For many, if not most laymen, religious affiliation and participation in the activities of churches have become thoroughly utilitarian. They believe quite pragmatically that religion "works," and they expect their churches and their ministers to serve *them*. There are levels of understanding and degrees of earnestness among church members. There must still be a considerable number of committed Christians who do not merely claim the benefits of Christian faith for themselves, but who also accept Christ's claim upon them.

Most laymen, however, still seem fixated at a level of

mediocrity that is even more mediocre than in Kierke-gaard's day, if such a thing is possible. Several varieties of interest and attachment can be distinguished here. The cult of mediocrity is no simple and unitary phenom-enon. It is compounded of subgroups, among which we may distinguish the cult of propriety, the cult of happi-ness, the cult of togetherness, the cult of tradition, and the cult of character-building. These groups are not mutually exclusive, and the same person may belong to two or more of them. Each of them has centered upon a more or less important product or by-product of Chris-tianity, which, when substituted for the centralities of Christian faith, becomes idolatrous. Each of them leads to mediocrity.

THE CULT OF PROPRIETY

Christianity is not opposed to propriety as such. Paul's comments on long-haired men and short-haired women are a part of Scripture (I Cor. 11:14–16), and indicate that social amenities have a place in the Christian per-spective of things. The proprieties and amenities of any society are definitive expressions of modesty and cour-tesy. Only when Christianity is reduced to proprieties and amenities, or when these are given precedence over "weightier matters of the law" do they become idolatrous.

Kierkegaard did not flout the proprieties. He conducted himself with circumspection and courtesy in personal relations. In spite of the scurrilous attacks of *The Corsair*, he was, as he himself said, decently and properly dressed. But he was not restrained by the proprieties from doing what he believed to be right. His attack upon the de-ceased Bishop Martensen within a few months of the old gentleman's death was certainly in poor taste. What he said about the bishop was true, however, and he felt that it must be said. We have prophetic souls in American Protestantism, but few, if any, who would be so brutally honest.

American Protestants are nice people. One of my friends, in the years of his childhood and youth, had never entered a church building. His parents were scientists, university teachers who had nothing to do with religion. When my friend became a student in another university three thousand miles from home, he missed his family and the refined companionship of family friends. He confessed his loneliness in a letter to his mother. His mother replied that, while it might sound like strange advice coming from her, if her son wanted to meet nice people, he might try going to church. On the following Sunday my friend attended a church service for the first time in his life. In the narthex of that Boston church he was cordially greeted by a friendly man and was ushered to a seat. After the service the same friendly man invited him to attend a Sunday school class of which this gentleman was the teacher. There the young man met others of his own age. After the class the same gentleman invited the young man home with him for Sunday dinner. And there, on that memorable day, my friend met the young woman who was to become his wife. Besides living happily ever after, my friend became a Christian, and years after, when I knew him, a very earnest and active one. Having spoiled my illustration by this last admission, I would like to return to my point: our churches are filled with nice people.

There is, of course, nothing wrong with this. I like to meet nice people too and have them for my friends. The trouble is that with many church members this is the meaning of the church. It is an institution for observing and promoting the amenities of life. This was the attitude back of the comment I quoted in Chapter Two: "Dr. 'Jones' is ruining our church with the kind of people he's bringing into it." The average middle-class church is composed of the proper people—people suited by income and cultural background to be members of that particular church.

With such people, and in the society of which they are a part, belonging to a church is one of the proprieties. It is on a par with keeping one's lawn mowed and one's clothes neatly pressed. When people who don't "fit" get into such a church through an excess of evangelistic zeal on someone's part, they rather quickly catch on, and either drop out of the church entirely or transfer to another congregation in which, with their clothes, tastes, and manners, they feel more at home. Members of the cult of propriety accept this situation, not only complacently, but with approval. This is Christianity!

THE CULT OF HAPPINESS

Our generation of Americans includes enough neurotics to form solid lines connecting all the psychiatric clinics in the country, and this feat could be accomplished without the familiar device of laying them end to end. Most of us are more or less neurotic, it seems. It is hardly normal anymore to be normal. Millions of people are maladjusted to the life they must live and are anxious about themselves.

Some years ago, an American businessman took a representative of Amtorg, the Soviet Union's purchasing and sales agency in this country, on a visit to Coney Island. For several hours the Russian visitor watched the hectic efforts of thousands of Americans to have fun. At the conclusion of the excursion, the American host asked the Russian, "Well, what do you think of it?" The Russian visitor replied, "What an unhappy people you must be!"

Coney Island is now, of course, plebian and passé. Americans are flocking in ever-increasing numbers to nightclubs and resorts—to Miami, Hot Springs, and Las Vegas. They are also flocking to the churches, and the reason in many cases is the same: they want to be happy. For the devotees of the cult of happiness, religion is primarily designed to give them some kind of emotional release from tension, anxiety, and frustration.

Perhaps more than any other of the pseudo-Christian cultists, the seekers after happiness are attempting to *use* God for their own purposes. God is "the man upstairs," friendly, undemanding, always ready to help, and omnipotent. Will Herberg seizes upon the phrase used by a psychiatrist to characterize God: "man's omnipotent servant." Faith is conceived by these religionists as "a sure-fire device to get what we want." (*Op. cit.*, p. 285.)

What people want, and therefore believe will make them happy, of course, varies widely with individuals. Often the goal is "success." No one on the American religious scene has so catered to the idea that successful people will be happy, and happy people will be successful, as has Norman Vincent Peale. Dr. Peale's thesis is that everyone can be both happy and successful if only he has the right attitude. One hesitates to add to the flood of caustic criticism that has surged up in reaction to his caricature of Christianity. Peale reduces success to a formula: "Pray hard, work hard, believe hard—and picture hard" (from a sermon by Dr. Peale quoted in Eckardt, *op. cit.*, p. 79). If only one pictures to himself what he would like to be, and then musters all his own energies and all the resources of faith, he can become what he wants to become. This is not only not true; it is the antithesis of Christianity.

What we are here concerned for is not to excoriate Dr. Peale, but to point out that he is exploiting an aspect of human nature which is there to be exploited. Man is by nature self-centered and inclined to be narcissistic. It is easy for him to fall into the error of losing his life by his own overanxious concern to save it. The pressures and fears of our time provide abundant occasion for people to be morbidly solicitous about their own personal welfare and adequacy. Many feel unable to meet the demands of society in general and of their own social situations in particular. They do not measure up to their own image of themselves as competent persons—self-assured and successful. They are frustrated and anxious; they feel guilty; they need help.

To these people Christ still calls, "Come to me, all who labor and are heavy-laden" (Matt. 11:28). But he also says, "If any man would come after me, let him deny himself and take up his cross and follow me" (Matt. 16:24). It would seem clear that no one can know the peace that Christ gives without also paying the price that he exacts. But people do not want to pay the price; they want an easy gospel, not a hard one.

I once entered the pastor's study of a church in which I was to preach, to find an adult Sunday school class in session. They were discussing the adult curriculum series that they were currently using, and a considerable group in the class were quite vocal in their criticism of the series. These people were saying, in effect, "We want Sunday school lessons we enjoy, with thoughts that make us happy, not lessons that make things seem more gloomy than we think they really are." They had been studying Jeremiah, and their complaint is understandable. But they were forgetting that the whole of Christianity is not contained in the "Hallelujah Chorus." That same God who said to the great unknown prophet of the sixth century B.C.: "Comfort, comfort my people" (Isa. 40:1), also said to Jeremiah, "Do not pray for this people, or lift up a cry or prayer on their behalf" (Jer. 11:14). The Bible is a book of hope; it is also a book of judgment on man's sin. The gospel of Christ is "good news," but it is realistic about man's wickedness.

We can expect that there will be millions of ordinary people who do not "buy" this. They do not want the whole gospel, but only those parts of it which are sweetness and light. Their approach to religion can be described as pragmatic, but it doesn't really work. It is utilitarian, but the utility of positive thinking for this purpose is extremely limited. Even the greatest of the utilitarian philosophers discovered that happiness is not a goal that can be successfully pursued. It is a by-product that comes most readily to those who are least concerned for it for themselves. Psychologically or theologically the devotees of the cult of happiness are doomed to disappointment. This is not the way to happiness—and it is not the Way.

THE CULT OF TOGETHERNESS

Human nature is gregarious, and Americans are very human. In this they are, perhaps, not different from other peoples. However, in this generation of Americans, something new has been added—the massive trend to conformity to which we have previously referred. Christianity, as we have seen, is an individual faith. Since unconscious, uncritical conformity leads to loss of individuality, conformity leads away from Christianity. Men do not become Christians en masse. Kierkegaard has much to say about this and emphasizes that a Christian relationship to God is discovered and carried on in solitariness. Every man must "fear and tremble" for himself, and make his own unconditional surrender to God's will and his own leap of faith.

It is amusing to contemplate what Kierkegaard would say if he could observe the American churches today. Claire Cox has given an interesting description of the wide variety of "fellowship" activities in churches across the nation "from Bible study to gourmet suppers." These include baby-sitting services, recreation rooms for the aged, and TV dens for teen-agers. Miss Cox continues:

> There are new attractions too: hot rod clubs, classes in good grooming, boy-girl discussions, barbecues, garden projects and coffee hours....
>
> The simplest form of fellowship is quite naturally the most popular—the "coffee break" after Sunday service. The Protestant Council of the City of New York conducted a survey to find out just how important the coffee hour was. It learned that this relatively simple event had become an important missionary tool in Manhattan churches, which found that their congregations regarded it as an ideal way to evangelize visitors. The parishioners also acknowledged that they enjoyed themselves. (Claire Cox, *The New-Time Religion*, pp. 166–167).

The First Baptist Church of Dallas, with twelve thousand members, has a separate, seven-story building, five floors of which are used for parking, and two for a gymnasium, bowling lanes with automatic pinsetters, and a skating rink. Activities in this church include courses in charm and modeling, beauty culture, cake-decorating, millinery, Bible study, and leather craft. There is a full-time "minister of recreation" who has a secretary and several paid, part-time assistants.

This is only one example of the efforts of today's churches to provide "togetherness." Many of the activities are in themselves good, and render important and helpful service to individuals and communities. But in many such activities, the purpose of the church is lost sight of, and many people are brought into the membership *merely* for fun and fellowship.

If these activities are defended as a subtle approach to evangelism, one may raise two questions: (1) Is a church descending here to the dubious ethical level of the "soft sell," or worse still, of the "hidden persuaders"? (2) What kind of members will they be who are attracted to the church through these methods? I am reminded of the now ancient and perhaps hackneyed quotation from Sam Jones, a late-nineteenth-century evangelist, to the effect that some people paraphrase Matt. 16:24 to read: "If any man would come after me, let him enjoy himself and take up his ice cream freezer and follow me."

The spirit of shallow good fellowship is not the spirit of Christ. Yet it is the only spirit that animates the religious activities of a large segment of the Protestant church membership. It may, in a superficial way, help people to adjust to one another. It does not reconcile man to God. Its gay and nonchalant spirit is aptly described by Miss Cox in her chapter title, "Praise the Lord and Pass the Coffee" (*ibid.*, p. 166).

THE CULT OF TRADITION

Little needs to be said descriptively about the devotees of the cult of tradition. Theirs is a well-known pattern of motivation. Christianity is the faith of their fathers, but it is not "living still," at least not in them. These people clutter the membership rolls of every church with any history. Some of them attend church regularly, some occasionally, some never. But this particular church is their church, even if it is only the church they stay away from. Theirs is an idolatrous attachment to the church's past or to the church building.

Sometimes they have moved to the suburbs and travel miles through city traffic once a week to attend services in "the old church." It is of the nature of their attachment to the church that they are opposed to change. They are stubbornly belligerent about any adjustments of the program of the church for more effective outreach to the inner-city neighborhood in which their church may now find itself. Like the exiled Hebrews of Ezekiel's time, they have not learned that God is portable; for them he is present and can be worshiped only "in Jerusalem."

In town and country churches these traditionalists maintain a type of nineteenth-century evangelistic piety that does not communicate to a twentieth-century generation. Within the framework of their limited perspective, many of these good people are serious Christians. They are what we often describe as "salt of the earth," using Jesus' phrase with considerable elasticity, or perhaps misusing it. But their hidebound traditionalism guarantees a standard of mediocrity from which most of the available ministerial leadership lacks the vision and/ or the ability to move them.

The Cult of Character-Building

In the United States the Sunday school has become a standard feature of the program of virtually every Protestant church. It has become the main reliance of American Protestantism for the religious education of children, youth, and adults. In some churches it has achieved a surprising level of educational effectiveness. In most, however, the teachers are ill-trained and halfhearted, the teaching is ill informed and dull, and the learning, Christianly speaking, is nil.

Yet the purpose of securing religious training for their children is probably the most widely operative motive among young parents for uniting with a church, attending its services, and joining in its activities. With a certain limited earnestness they desire Christian education for their offspring, and Sunday school and youth groups are valued for the same reason that Boy Scouts and Campfire Girls are valued. In these days of widespread juvenile (and adult) delinquency, parents feel the need of all the help they can get to bring their children up to be decent, law-abiding members of society.

Those who become church members for this reason do not necessarily or even usually become Christians. With a certain earnestness they go through the motions of being church members. They attend services and accept responsibilities in church programs. They are to be commiserated with rather than blamed for their limited awareness of the true nature of the Christian faith. Worthy though their motives are, they cannot be expected to be more than mediocre Christians. They have no inwardness in their own lives. They believe in Christianity, but not in Christ. They often have great faithfulness, but no faith, in the Christian meaning of that term.

In large part it is these people who teach Sunday school classes and serve as department superintendents and youth leaders. We should not presume to limit the Holy Spirit, but it would seem obvious that they are not likely to communicate a faith they do not have. They are not only mediocre Christians themselves; they make the educational programs of many churches production lines of mediocrity.

THE HIGH CALLING

There is nothing mediocre about the Protestant faith. It is a high faith and a demanding one. Truly understood, it calls forth our best and assures us of God's guidance and power to achieve that of which our best is incapable. In Protestantism, faith is not a substitute for good works; it is the attitude of faith that makes good works possible.

Few laymen understand the true nature of Christianity. It is with mistaken sincerity that they identify it with limited types of folk religion. This is partly due to ignorance. It is also partly due to human sinfulness, which prefers man's way to God's way. Ways that are traditional and familiar, ways that promise much at little cost— these will always appeal to many. There will always be purveyors, also, of a watered-down gospel, ministers who are willing to give people what they want in order to make a show of results. Laymen should be warned by Kierkegaard's monologue on a character in one of Holberg's plays:

> After all, Stundenstrup is clearly in the right about the Town Hall, that it is a very handsome building, and that for the song at which these "honest men" are willing to dispose of it, it is the most brilliant transaction that can well be imagined. This must be conceded by his paternal uncle at the town of Thy, by all the kindred in Salling, and by all shrewd men wherever they are.
>
> What Stundenstrup neglected to consider was whether these honest men stood in such a relation to the Town Hall that they were able to dispose of it. If not, then the price, if it were only four shillings and sixpence, would be very dear—for the Town Hall. So then, cheapness is not to be extolled unconditionally; it has its

limits: if one does not get the thing one buys for an incredibly low price, the price is not cheap but very dear.

So it is with Christianity. That an eternal blessedness is an inestimable good, far more considerable than the Town Hall, and if it can be bought for the song at which the priests dispose of it, it may be considered a far, far, far more brilliant transaction that that of Stundenstrup's in buying the Town Hall—that I am willing to concede. (*Attack*, pp. 50–51.)

To believe that what one gets at any price less than everything one is and has is really Christianity is to be deceived and cheated. If Kierkegaard's warning has a hollow ring (and it will) to many readers, it may be that the creeping materialism of contemporary society has destroyed your faith in the reality of life after death, or it may be that you are thinking of eternal blessedness in terms of "pie in the sky when you die." Consistently in the New Testament, eternity includes life after death, but it also includes the life you live now. It is not a state of being for which you must wait until you enter a speculative hereafter. It is abundant life now—abundant life that does not end at death but continues into a blessed eternity.

To attain this feeling of eternal blessedness had been a struggle for Kierkegaard. He had been a Christian for ten years before he could write with authenticity about it. But it was very real to him in his struggle with the established church. Denounced and vilified by many, and supported by very few, he yet lived with a deepening inner peace.

This is the peace which passes understanding, and it is not purchased lightly. It is the free gift of God to those who will receive it. But it is found and possessed only by those who are willing to live, morally and spiritually, in a strait and narrow way.

Sophisticated in worldly ways, Americans are a comically unsophisticated people in matters of the spirit. Most Americans are not consciously hypocrites or heretics. Kierkegaard's estimate can, I think, be fairly applied: "For one certified hypocrite there are 100,000 twaddlers; for one certified heretic, 100,000 nincompoops" (*Attack*, p. 108).

The state of lay Christianity is, I think, worse than in Kierkegaard's time. Laymen are spiritually illiterate, sometimes willfully so. It doesn't occur to them to question the genuineness of the counterfeit currency that freely passes as coin of the realm in American church life. On some kind of easy-payment plan the average Protestant proposes to purchase his own small place in God's Kingdom. Typically, he doesn't expect too much—indeed, he doesn't expect enough. With the bread of life available, he is complacently content with stale crumbs.

Unaware of the richness of his Protestant heritage, he is willing to forfeit his rights and responsibilities under the doctrine of "the priesthood of all believers," if his minister will, with equal complacency, serve as his hired priest. The phrase "the recovery of the laity," which is in current use among us, must become an urgent goal. One of our present dangers is that, having verbalized it so neatly in this phrase, we shall think we have accomplished it. We haven't—it is one of the great unfinished tasks of Protestantism. As Protestants we must work at it as though our lives depended on it, because they do!

CHAPTER SIX

Worship Is a Sham

FOR MOST PEOPLE Christianity is still, as it was for Kierkegaard's Bishop Mynster, a Sunday religion. With apparent zeal and earnestness, Mynster proclaimed an evangelical faith from the pulpit, and led his congregation in the Church of Our Lady in solemn worship. On Monday all of this was discarded in favor of business as usual.

The basic difficulty, with both nineteenth-century Danes and twentieth-century Americans, is that although we all profess in our worship that we want to please God, we haven't the slightest intention of doing so in our daily living. Kierkegaard's fable of "The Tame Geese" is directed at this fundamental dishonesty. Let us suppose, he says, that geese could talk, and that they came together every Sunday for divine worship, and one of the ganders preached.

The essential content of the sermon was: what a lofty destiny the geese had, what a high goal the Creator (and every time this word was mentioned the geese curtsied and the ganders bowed the head) had set before the geese; by the aid of wings they could fly away to distant regions, blessed climes, where properly they were at home, for here they were only strangers.

So it was every Sunday. And as soon as the assembly broke up each waddled home to his own affairs. And then the next Sunday again to divine worship and then

89

again home—and that was the end of it, they throve and were well-liking, became plump and delicate—and then were eaten on Martinmas Eve—and that was the end of it.

That was the end of it. For though the discourse sounded so lofty on Sunday, the geese on Monday were ready to recount to one another what befell a goose that had wanted to make serious use of the wings the Creator had given him, designed for the high goal that was proposed to him—what befell him, what a terrible death he encountered. This the geese could talk about knowingly among themselves. But, naturally, to speak about it on Sundays was unseemly; for, said they, it would then become evident that our divine worship is really only making a fool of God and of ourselves.

Among the geese there were, however, some individuals which seemed suffering and grew thin. About them it was currently said among the geese: There you see what it leads to when flying is taken seriously. For because their hearts are occupied with the thought of wanting to fly, therefore they become thin, do not thrive, do not have the grace of God as we have who therefore become plump and delicate.

And so the next Sunday they went again to divine worship, and the old gander preached about the high goal the Creator (here again the geese curtsied and the ganders bowed the head) had set before the geese, whereto the wings were designed.

So with the divine worship of Christendom. Man also has wings, he has imagination. (Walter Lowrie, *op. cit.*, pp. 544–545.)

In every church in Christendom, we who call ourselves Christians go through this farcical ritual every Sunday, and nobody notices how funny it is. In every congregation there are, perhaps, a few sincere worshipers. Who can know their number? But it is also obvious that millions of "worshipers" repeat the words, "Thy will be done, on earth as it is in heaven," without the slightest concern for God's will except as it may happen to coincide with their own wills.

It was Kierkegaard's insistence that the ideals praised and professed in worship ought to be faithfully and visibly expressed in daily life. It would seem to be a reasonable requirement; yet we do not do it. We pursue gain rather than God. We make our plans and decisions with consideration only for the political, economic, and gregarious concerns of life at the human-social level. We want status, reputation, power, and influence. We want to be comfortable. We want friends. We want pleasure. We do not choose to live sacrificially. The last thing we would think of doing is to give all or venture all for Christ. We profess to admire and serve a higher wisdom, but we live by the wisdom of the world. When anyone does otherwise we regard him as a fanatic or a fool.

We neither love our enemies nor pray for them. It would be outrageously poor judgment to turn the other cheek, or to give one's "cloak as well" (Matt. 5:39–40). We don't forgive the wrongs done us; we call our lawyer, and have him sue for damages. We spend our lives laying up treasures, even if only through Social Security. We continually try to serve two masters, and we live in an anxiety that has learned nothing from the birds and the lilies. Of course most of us do not steal, and we lie only in harmless ways. Only a few of us commit adultery; but many of us covet, though our wealth is no longer counted in terms of oxen and asses.

Probably it is inevitable, or at least predictable, that our lives will be tainted and tarnished by the earthly and earthy concerns of the society of which we are members. For all of us some compromise is necessary if we are to live normal lives. What Kierkegaard demanded was an honest admission that our lives are a compromise, that we do not live by the Christianity of the New Testament. Most professing Christians are reluctant to admit the wide discrepancy between the ideals they profess and the attitudes and habits of their daily living. They go to church and worship in Pharisaic self-righteousness. To confess their sins and repent of them would do irreparable damage to the false self-image with which they face the world.

Protestantism abolished the confessional. There were some good reasons for this; but the unfortunate result has been that for most Protestants there is no awareness of sin, no repentance, no aspiration to a better life, no experience of God's forgiving grace, and no improvement of character and of life. Most Protestants are, therefore, poorly prepared to worship.

OUR MAN-CENTERED WORSHIP

Protestants have lost the sense of worship as an end in itself. We do not make an offering of ourselves and our worship to Almighty God. At best our worship is almost completely self-oriented. It does not occur to us that worship is primarily an opportunity for us to glorify God, and that "man's chief end is to glorify God, and to enjoy him forever" (*Westminster Shorter Catechism*). We are not especially concerned for the glory of God, and we do not know him well enough to enjoy him. The typical Protestant experience of worship is man-centered. Roman Catholics have the advantage that their experience of worship is unmistakably God-centered.

In man-centered worship the purpose of the worshiper is to get something from worship. At the lowest level of such "worship," the worshiper goes to church to be seen, i.e., to be known as a churchgoer, to wear and show off fashionable clothes, to move in or move into the desired social circles, or to establish contacts that will enhance his prestige or advance his career.

The new proprietor of a market in a middle-class Chicago neighborhood attended several churches with his family, and after a few weeks of "shopping" united with a Congregational church. When asked by the pastor why he had chosen the Congregational church, the businessman replied with complete candor, "Yours was the only church in _____ Park that didn't have a grocer in its membership."

Most man-oriented worship has, I hope, more worthy motives. Protestants go to church because they feel the need of help in bearing life's pressures and meeting its problems. They need to "have their batteries recharged." They need the assurances of Scripture and the messages of guidance, courage, and hope, which are the responsibility of the man in the pulpit. They need the fellowship of Christian believers, of friends with shared convictions, purposes, and ideals. In such worship the worshiper is concerned for himself; he worships for his own good.

In God-oriented worship, on the other hand, the worshiper is concerned for God in the sense that he feels it is important to God that men should worship him. This is Scriptural: "True worshipers will worship the Father in spirit and truth, *for such the Father seeks to worship him*" (John 4:23). (The italics are, of course, ours.) God *seeks* worshipers, and sincere worship is acceptable and pleasing to him. Worship at its best is a genuine expression of awe, reverence, and gratitude. It is an act of dedication. The typical Protestant has little awareness of this.

To offer himself as a "living sacrifice, holy and acceptable to God," is farthest from his thought. He goes to church, not to give, but to receive.

The worshiper who goes to the sanctuary with *his* own desires, *his* purposes, *his* petitions, gets in his own way. If what he really wants is to come closer to God, to serve him in purity and newness of life, and to be strengthened for this service, a worshiper must begin with confession of sin and the humble, repentant offering of himself. In worship, as in life, a Christian must seek first the Kingdom of God before other things can be added.

The self-oriented worshiper, seeking happiness, or praying that things may be the way he thinks they should be, is trying to *use* God in what never succeeds in being worship. God will not be used, and it is childish for men to suppose that they *can* use him in this or any other way. Paradoxically, it is those who worship for the glory of God, seeking nothing for themselves, who receive most. Not seeking peace of mind, they achieve it; asking nothing for themselves, they receive much; humbly confessing their own inability to stand alone, they walk with God.

He who worships God in spirit and in truth must worship in utter humility, knowing that he deserves nothing at God's hand. Humility is born in awareness of our own unworthiness, in repentance for our sins and our continuing sinfulness. Repentance is not the act of a moment; it is a way of life. Many of us have moments of truth when we view our natural selves in a mirror (James 1:23). We know what we are and what we have done, and are sorry. But we suffer from amnesia, we forget what we do not wish to remember, and our repentance fades. Kierkegaard distrusted sudden repentance.

Sudden repentance would drink down all the bitterness of sorrow in a single draught and then hurry on. It wants to get away from guilt. It wants to banish all recollection of it, fortifying itself by imagining that it does this in order not to be held back in the pursuit of the Good. It is its wish that guilt, after a time, might be wholly forgotten. And once again, this is impatience. Perhaps a later sudden repentance may make it apparent that the former sudden repentance lacked true inwardness. (*Purity of Heart*, p. 16.)

S. K. goes on to point out that "in the temporal, and sensual, and social sense, repentance is in fact something that comes and goes during the years. But in the eternal sense, it is a silent daily anxiety" (*ibid.*). Kierkegaard lived in this daily, humble, repentant concern. Professor Rasmus Nielsen, of the University of Copenhagen, was the only member of the Theological Faculty who had any appreciation of Kierkegaard's ability and contribution. But Nielsen overdid it; his praise was so adulatory as to be embarrassing. S. K. sent for Nielsen, and scuttled his unwelcome praise, apparently with effectiveness. What the whole conversation was we have no way of knowing, but S. K.'s report is: "I said as solemnly as possible to him: I am a penitent" (*Journals*, p. 427). Søren Kierkegaard lived his entire life from 1838 on as a penitent, and his penitence deepened as he drew nearer to God in spiritual awareness.

The average service of Protestant worship is carried on with scant attention to the act of repentance and confession. Even when a prayer of confession is included in the order of worship, it is likely to be a mere formality; for the average Protestant American is not a penitent, nor is he humble before God. The scandal of our public worship of God is that while our prayers and our hymns may express repentance, faith, and gratitude, our attitudes and our lives do not.

We can worship God only as we stand in awe of him. In our generation, Americans stand in awe of nothing. We can worship God only as we truly love him. Brash, spiritually underprivileged, and ignorant, the average American Protestant does not know what it means to love God. He "joined the church" at age twelve or thirteen because his friends also were joining. He received only perfunctory instruction in the great truths of the Christian faith. He may have attended Sunday school regularly, but he learned nothing that was related to his own life.

When he left his parental home to work elsewhere, or to fulfill his military obligations, or to go to college, he severed the only ties that bound him to the church. In college, if he had this privilege, he may have learned much, but he learned nothing about Christianity. After some years, married and with small children of his own, he and his wife sought out a church, or were brought in by the church's outreach. His wife, perhaps, was able to get a letter of dismission from her home church, and both of them united with the new church, he on reaffirmation of a faith in Christ that he never had. His religion is a vague, moralistic pietism. God is an equally vague, hypothetical, grandfatherly character who rewards his children when they are good and shrugs his shoulders and smiles indulgently when they are bad.

This kind of "Christian" knows nothing of Christianity as a demanding faith or as a religion of suffering or of repentance and redemption. The only demand exerted upon his life is that of a fairly comfortable conformity.

And Christianity at the level of suffering is beyond his comprehension. Quite understandably, he doesn't go along with this business of suffering. The whole effort of our "humanitarian" idealism and of any "civilized" society is toward the elimination of suffering. Only criminals should be made to suffer, and even this is now regarded as dubious penology. And obviously, Mr. Average Protestant is not a criminal—or is he? In any case he has no real understanding of what it means to be a Christian; and if he has any inkling of what it will cost him, he will be reluctant to learn.

It is such people who enter our sanctuaries to worship. Most of them are "good people." Some who are not so good manage to maintain an appearance of respectability in a church that is no longer nosy about the private lives of its members. Intent upon other and "more important" affairs, these people are only peripherally concerned with the affairs of the Kingdom of God. On Sundays, however, many of them regularly go to their churches to "worship."

In this chapter, up to now, we have said that the public worship of God in American Protestant churches is a sham for two reasons. One is that the daily lives of the worshipers do not correspond to the faith they ostensibly profess on Sunday. Since life in the world is what it is, this discrepancy between faith and life, humanly speaking, is inevitable. A second reason, therefore, for the sham and shame of our worship is its man-oriented nonchalance, its seeking from God what we have not put ourselves in a position to receive, its disregard of sin and the need for repentance and forgiveness. For many, and perhaps most, Protestant churchgoers, worship is not true worship.

The Sacrament of Baptism

The comedy of Protestant churches reaches its climax in the administration of the sacraments. Kierkegaard felt deeply about this and is even more violent, therefore, than he is on other subjects. Though he was a Lutheran, he seems to be moving away from Lutheranism in two directions, both of which would be anathematized by devout and orthodox members of that faith. For those who administer the sacraments, the clergy, he turns toward the Roman Catholic position of clerical celibacy. On the subject of Baptism, he becomes a Baptist, not in advocating immersion, but in adopting the much more essential Baptist doctrine of believers' baptism.

The practice of infant baptism was certainly abused in the Danish Lutheran Church, and it continues to be abused in American churches today. Kierkegaard depicts baptism as a sort of two-act comedy. In the first act, a young father who has no religious convictions or proclivities is prevailed upon by tradition, circumstances, his wife (still exhausted from the lying-in), and the priest to have his child baptized. So the father becomes, for the time being, an evangelical Lutheran. He persuades some of his agnostic friends to serve as godfathers who will promise to help bring up the child as a Christian! An appointment is made with the priest, the midwife brings the baby, a young woman holds its bonnet "coquettishly," and the silk-robed priest "with a graceful gesture sprinkles water three times on the dear little baby and dries his hands gracefully with a towel."

> And this they dare to present to God under the name of Christian Baptism. Baptism—it was with this sacred ceremony the Savior of the world was consecrated for

his life's work, and after him the disciples, men who had well reached the age of discretion and who then, dead to this life . . . , promised to be willing to live as sacrificed men in this world of falsehood and evil. (*Attack,* p. 205.)

Kierkegaard, in doubtful taste, points up the comical in the situation by suggesting that "the young lady, instead of holding a little bonnet sentimentally over the baby, . . . satirically . . . hold a nightcap over the presumptive father. For to have religion in that way is . . . a pitiful comedy" (*ibid.,* p. 206).

The second act of the comedy is not given in this immediate context by Kierkegaard, but it does not misrepresent him to bring the two acts together. The second act of the comedy is confirmation.

> "The tender infant," says "Christendom," "cannot personally take the baptismal vow. . . ." And so . . . they have chosen the period from fourteen to fifteen years of age, the age of boyhood. . . . This real person—there can be no objection, he's man enough to undertake to perform the baptismal vows made in behalf of the tender infant.
>
> A boy of fifteen! In case it were a question of ten dollars the father would say, "No, my boy, that can't be left to your discretion, you're not yet dry behind the ears." But as for his eternal blessedness . . .—for that the age of fifteen years is the most appropriate.
>
> The most appropriate—ah, yes, if, as was previously remarked, divine worship is assumed to have a double aim: in a delicate way . . . to treat God as a fool; and to give occasion for family festivities. . . .
>
> The whole thing is a comedy—and taking this view of it, perhaps something might be done to introduce more dramatic illusion into this solemnity, as, for example, if

a prohibition were published against anyone being confirmed in a jacket, *item* an ordinance that upon the floor of the church male confirmants must wear a beard, which of course could fall off at the family festivities in the evening, and perhaps be used for fun and jest. (*Ibid.,* pp. 217–218.)

Customs have changed, and the current practices of Protestant denominations vary greatly. Kierkegaard's criticisms are, however, still valid. Whether you belong to a church that practices infant baptism, or one that practices believers' baptism, my friend, you probably belong to a church that makes a mockery of the sacrament. This is not to say that baptism is never administered and received with utter sincerity. It often, perhaps usually, is taken seriously by ministers, by adults being baptized, and by parents who present their children for baptism. But, like all other practices of American Protestantism, baptism has become part of our folkways.

It is the respectable thing to do, either to have your children baptized if you are a Presbyterian, etc., or to encourage them to be baptized at an early age if you are a Baptist. It is probably more fashionable to be an Episcopalian, and have your infant christened! However this may be, the consequence is that many comparatively young children, even in immersionist churches, present themselves for baptism at an age when, as S. K. would say, they couldn't even be trusted with ten dollars. And many parents present infants for baptism or christening whose relation to the church is extremely tenuous. They themselves have little real faith. Their vow to rear their children as Christians is halfhearted, and the effectiveness of their compliance with such a vow is nil.

Serious questions can, of course, be raised about infant baptism. It has validity, perhaps, as a time-honored and meaningful practice of the church. It ill becomes any denomination to take a legalistic stand for its own particular practice of baptism. What is a sacrament? If we reply that a sacrament is a practice instituted by Christ as "an outward and visible sign of an inward and spiritual grace," it is necessary to point out, for example, that Christ did not institute infant baptism. Or at least there is no record that he did. He loved little children, and took them in his arms and blessed them; so far as we know, he did not baptize them, or leave any instruction that they should be baptized.

For that matter, it is clear that he did not originate the practice of baptism. Its use as a symbol for spiritual cleansing antedates the days of his ministry. He accepted it, however, as symbolic of his own human dedication to his divine mission, and, as our risen Lord, he commanded that those who become his followers should be baptized. Theological argument about the mode of baptism is beside the point; and perhaps S. K. would also admit that it is not infant baptism or teen-age confirmation to which he is so violently opposed.

The point, Kierkegaard's and mine, is that it is not the practice of baptism that is wrong (by whatever mode or at whatever age), but the meaningless practice of baptism or of any other rite or ordinance of the church. When the covenant that baptism symbolizes is not entered into with earnest and genuine dedication, it becomes a sin. All the forms, the dignity and solemnity, with which a church surrounds it cannot redeem it from dishonesty.

The test of the genuineness of infant baptism, therefore, is the Christian commitment of parents and the integrity of intent with which they represent their child at the altar of God, and seek his grace and guidance in performing their task as Christian parents. These are admittedly difficult matters for a minister to determine. Nor is he in a position to refuse baptism for children of parents who are members in good standing in his church. Our basic difficulty here is statistical Christianity and our padded church rolls.

A further point that Kierkegaard makes is that our whole procedure for bringing children and young people into the church can degenerate into a sort of religious exploitation. The number of people who unite with churches on confession of faith after age sixteen is a rapidly declining one for each subsequent year of individual age. After age thirty there are very few who unite with a church for the first time. From the standpoint of sheer self-interest, Protestant ministers and churches have a considerable stake in maintaining the Protestant birthrate, baptism rate, and confirmation rate. If we do not maintain these, we will, statistically speaking, lose ground. As Kierkegaard points out:

> If the decision with regard to religion is postponed to the mature age of man . . . , many would perhaps have character enough not to want to be feignedly Christian. Hence the priest seeks to take possession of people in young and tender years, so that in maturer years they might have the difficulty of breaking a "sacred" obligation, imposed, to be sure, in boyhood, but which many perhaps may feel superstitious about breaking. (*Ibid.*, p. 218.)

It would be a harsh thing if I would venture to suggest that the clergy today may be moved by similar motives. Are their efforts to baptize and confirm as many children and young people as possible motivated as much by worldly wisdom as by zeal for the salvation of souls? No members, no job! And the age at which people can be gotten into the church in droves is while they are too young to realize fully what they are letting themselves in for. Is the real zeal here for maintaining the statistics, and the budget, and the prestige? I judge no one, and I accuse no one. These are merely questions "for self-examination," which a minister may use if he chooses to do so.

Parents are, of course, collaborators in this shepherding (or herding) operation. It would be highly unsuccessful without them. Drafted themselves into the army of the Lord at an early age, they have good precedent for this way of doing it; it seems to them the proper thing to do. Even though their relationship to the church is peripheral, even though they have no deep conviction of the truth of Christianity, even though they may no longer believe that there is a heaven or a hell, they want their children to have the insurance policy that goes with the "enlistment," just in case! So Johnny and Mary join the communicants class and are willingly or reluctantly shepherded into the fold; or should we say that they are marched—*one*, two, three, four, *one*, two, three, four— into the church of Jesus Christ? They take up their cross and follow him! Is it any wonder that about one third of them discard said cross when they discover for themselves that it is heavy, and another one third store it away as inconspicuously as possible in the "utility room" of their lives, unwilling to throw it away, but also unwilling to bear it?

From the staid christening-to-confirmation of the high churchmen to the revivalistic social pressure of the rural Southern Baptist or the emotional hysteria of the Holiness groups, by hook or by crook, we get our young people into the church. And the act of receiving them, be it believers' baptism or confirmation, we call Christian worship. Is it?

The Table of the Lord

No one could regard the sacrament of the Lord's Supper with deeper, more genuine piety than this Lutheran layman, Søren Kierkegaard. When, in 1838, as a young man of twenty-five, he returned to Christianity after a few years of living as an irresponsible aesthete, he symbolized this return by receiving Communion in the cathedral Church of Our Lady, alone and by appointment. In the years that followed he had continued to be a regular communicant, and on his deathbed he expressed an earnest desire for the Communion, which, however, he would no longer accept at the hands of a priest of the state church.

A part of the literature of this last period of his life (1848–1855) is the group of addresses entitled "Discourses at the Communion on Fridays," which constitute the fourth section of *Christian Discourses*. In a *Journal* entry of the period, he notes that there is a sharp transition from the ironic probing into the hypocrisies of the church in Part III, "Thoughts Which Wound from Behind," to these ironic devotional addresses of Part IV.

Based on Matt. 11:28, "Come to me, all who labor and are heavy-laden, and I will give you rest," the second of these addresses raises the possibility that there are some people who are exempted from labor and care.

> Is it the meaning of the gospel when it invites all them that labor and are heavy-laden, that there are some . . . to whom this invitation does not apply because they are whole and have no need of a physician? . . . The gospel must be understood differently, it invites all; the gospel is unwilling to be a bypath, offering

comfort and consolation to certain persons in affliction. . . .

It requires that the invited guest shall in a deeper
sense labor and be heavy-laden. For there is a sorrow
unto God; it has to do with nothing earthly and temporal, not with thy outward circumstances, not with thy
future, it is unto God. He who bears this sorrow quietly
and humbly in his heart, he it is that labors. And there
is a heavy burden; no worldly power can lay it upon thy
shoulders, but neither can any man, any more than thou
thyself, take it off. It is guilt and the consciousness of
guilt, or still heavier, it is sin and the consciousness of
sin. He who bears this burden . . . is heavy-laden, but
precisely so, . . . as the gospel requires. And there is an
affliction, a deep, an eternal affliction; it has not to do
with thy outward circumstances, with thy lot in life. . . .
It has to do with thine actions, . . . precisely with those
actions which a man would prefer to have forgotten, for
it has to do with the actions whereby thou didst offend
against God or against other men, whether they be hidden or manifest. This affliction is penitence. He who
sighs penitently, yea, it is he that labors and is heavy-
laden. No one else labors so heavily, yet it is this precisely which the invitation of the gospel requires.

But the invitation of the gospel not only implies a
demand, it also announces a promise: "I will give you
rest for your souls." (*Christian Discourses,* pp. 270–
271.)

Quoting the lines of a familiar Danish hymn:

"Remind me, Jesu, yet again
Of all thine anguish and distress,
Remind me of thy soul's deep pain";

and I Cor. 11:23: "The Lord Jesus, on the night when he
was betrayed . . . ," Kierkegaard indicates that when

Christ left the upper room he went to meet pain, scorn, mockery, and death, yet he went with eagerness.

> When once they would acclaim him king, he fled, and when they come armed to seize him, he advances to meet them, saying, "Whom seek ye?" No doubt he once with a kiss hailed Judas as an apostle, nor does he refuse the kiss of Judas who, as he knows, would betray him. (*Ibid.*, p. 285.)

We are all betrayers potentially. It may indeed be true that I am not the kind of man who would skulk through the shadows of night feloniously betraying or ignominiously denying my Lord, or the kind who would join the rabble in the streets shouting, "Crucify him." Assuredly I would never join such a heartless, jeering throng as the one that surrounded the cross. I am the kind who will shrewdly remain at home, keeping myself out of it, and "letting my servant report" to me what has happened. Says Kierkegaard:

> I have seen "Love" betrayed, and I have understood something about myself, that I also am a man, and that to be a man is to be a sinful man. Not for this have I become a hater of men, least of all a hater of other men; but I never forget this night nor what I have understood about myself. He whom the race crucified was the Redeemer; just for this cause do I, as belonging to the race, feel the need of a redeemer.... From this moment I no longer trust myself, I will not let myself be deceived, as though I were better because I was not tried like those contemporaries. No, fearful of myself as I have become, I will seek refuge in him the Crucified. To him will I pray that he will deliver me from the evil, and deliver me from myself. Only as saved by him and in his company, when he holds me fast, do I know that I shall not betray him. (*Ibid.*, p. 287.)

Our emphasis upon the demanding character of the Christian faith is genuinely Kierkegaardian, but it should not obscure the emphasis that S. K. also made upon the reassurances of the Christian faith. Interpreting the text: "If we deny him, he also will deny us; if we are faithless, he remains faithful—for he cannot deny himself" (II Tim. 2:12–13), Kierkegaard notes the paradoxical nature of the statement. He comments that one who denies Christ is obviously unfaithful; but it is not necessarily true that one who is unfaithful also denies him. We, ourselves, do not deny him, but we are often unfaithful. He, however, remains faithful; he does not deny himself, i.e., he does not act in contradiction of the consistent, loving faithfulness of his own nature.

The first part of this text (II Tim. 2:12–13) is what S. K. calls "the stern word"; the second part is "the gentle word." He says in this particular Communion address that, by the very fact of their attendance at the Communion, his hearers are not denying Christ, but confessing him.

> Though it may be profitable that the stern word be brought to remembrance, be heard along with the other, as it certainly belongs with it, though we ought not to separate what God hath joined together in Christ, . . . from gentleness take away severity which is in it, from the gospel take away the law which is in it, from salvation take away perdition which is in it; yet surely it is the latter word which is preeminently appropriate for us to dwell upon today. . . .
>
> So in thy relationship with Him thou hast one concern the less, or rather one blessedness more than it is possible any man could ever have in his relationship with another man. In the relationship between two, every individual, humanly speaking, has constantly a double concern: he has it for himself, that he may now remain

faithful; ah, but at the same time he is concerned lest the other may not remain faithful. But . . . Jesus Christ remains faithful. Hence in this relationship the peace and blessedness of eternity is complete, thou hast only one concern, the concern for thyself, that thou mayest remain faithful—for he remains eternally faithful. (*Ibid.*, pp. 290–291.)

Kierkegaard points out that the sacrament of the Lord's Supper is for all sinners. The only requirement is that they take to the Sacrament with them the burden of their own sin and guilt. Christ excludes no one, but if I, through pride, rate myself as any better than the worst of sinners, and less deeply in need of deliverance, I exclude myself. In my remembrance, I have failed to live again that night on which he was betrayed, realizing that I have no right to believe that, had I been there, I would be any stronger or more faithful than those disciples who failed him. Yet the Sacrament reminds me also that Christ went to meet Judas, and accepted his kiss; I must ask myself why I am here at the Lord's Table and what is my intention toward him.

So I will pray that he will deliver me from myself, and keep me faithful to him. I will hear "the stern word" and "the gentle word"; I will know that while I cannot trust my own faithfulness, I can trust his faithfulness, and so know the peace that he gives.

Few men have commented on the sacrament of the Lord's Supper with such clear and deep appreciation of its meaning. His criticisms were directed, not against the Sacrament, but against the attitudes and motives of both clergy and laity in its observance. The priests, he contended, were mere tradesmen performing the routine tasks of their trade for the sake of profit. Many lay people participated in the Sacrament from motives quite other than those of repentance, spiritual need, and gratitude. He describes a tradesman who thinks that he must be "just like all the other tradesmen," and who believes that the universal motto of tradesmen is: "Every man's a thief in his business."

As for religion—well, really his religion is this: Every man's a thief in his business. He also has a religion in addition to this, and his opinion is that especially every tradesman ought to have one. "A tradesman," says he, "even if he has no religion, ought never to let that be noticed, for that may readily be harmful to him by casting possible suspicion upon his honesty; and preferably a tradesman ought to have the religion which prevails in the land." . . .

So two or four times a year this man puts on his best clothes, and goes to Communion. Up comes a priest (like those that jump up out of a snuffbox when one touches a spring) who jumps up whenever he sees "a blue bank note." [A five-dollar bill.] And thereupon the priest celebrates the Holy Communion, from which the tradesman, or rather both tradesmen (. . . priest and honest citizen) return home to their customary way of life. . . .

And this is what one dares to offer to God under the name of the sacrament of the Lord's Supper, the Communion in Christ's body and blood! (*Attack*, pp. 206–207.)

The solemnity of the situation, says Kierkegaard, "is this: to live before and after in complete worldliness—and then a ceremony." This is, indeed, approximately the way we do it in twentieth-century America. We too live in complete worldliness, and then from time to time have a ceremony, the sacrament of the Lord's Supper, which makes everything all right. Or if it doesn't quite make everything all right, at least we are keeping up appearances, and among us Americans this is the important thing! After all, in his sacrifice upon the cross, Christ paid the price of our sins, paid them in full; that debt is liquidated once for all. This is what we celebrate in the Communion. We may still have to make payments on our homes, automobiles, TV sets, household appliances, etc., but salvation is free!

Of course we do pay something to the church; many of us use our convenient little envelopes for this every Sunday. On Communion Sundays in some of our churches, we also have a box in the narthex where those who love the poor *very* much, or who have especially guilty consciences, can put in a special offering—you know, a dollar bill or a five-dollar bill—for the "deacons' fund."

All Christ commanded in connection with this Sacrament was that we do it in remembrance of him. We do remember him; and our minister speaks quite feelingly about him. It's really quite impressive—makes us feel holy, sort of! We're reminded, too, that Paul said, "As often as ye eat this bread, and drink this cup, ye do show the Lord's death till he come" (I Cor. 11:26, KJV). We do show it, don't we? We make quite a show of it in some of our churches—beautiful music, vestments, Communion sets, silver chalices—we really go all out to show Christ and everyone else how much we honor him.

Of course this business about his coming again—showing "the Lord's death till he come"—is a little embarrassing. After all, it's been nearly two thousand years. Probably Paul and the other apostles were laboring under a slight misunderstanding about this. Some of us, when we think about it at all, have a suspicion that Christ isn't coming. Not that it matters; what matters really is that we remember him every Sunday or at least every three months. It doesn't matter that we forget him the rest of the time. Or does it?

Some who read this twentieth-century Kierkegaardian satire (if anyone does!) will feel that it is a caricature of clerical and lay attitudes in worship, and a very unfair one. If you feel this way, you have a right to your opinion. But read it again, and ponder it, my friend! Like Isaiah's contemporaries, we trample the courts of the Lord, but now as then, because of our patent insincerity, God hates our solemn assemblies. Like the Pharisee, we go up to the temple to pray, but we do not go down to our houses justified. Like Kierkegaard's Danish contemporaries, we Americans in much of our worship are engaged in the "unparalleled impudence" of "putting a wax nose on God" (*ibid.*, p. 212).

CHAPTER SEVEN

The Way Is Narrow

For us," said Kierkegaard, "there is but one salvation: Christianity. And verily for Christianity there is but one possible salvation: severity." (*Training in Christianity*, p. 222.) Our easygoing self-justification for our failure to measure up to the standards set by Christ for his followers calls indeed for severity. Christ pointed out that "the gate is narrow and the way is hard, that leads to life, and those who find it are few" (Matt. 7:14). From the time of his "second conversion" in Holy Week of 1848, Kierkegaard's whole effort was to confront men with the stark, uncompromising character of true Christianity.

S. K. realized full well that such a rigorous presentation of the Christian faith would repel many. They would be offended by the gospel; but this is not new, nor is it an undesirable situation. Any authentic presentation of the Christian faith will inevitably offend some people. Christianity is an offensive religion, not merely in the sense of being aggressive—offensive rather than defensive—but also in the sense that from New Testament times on many have been offended by it. It was "a stumbling-block to Jews and folly to Gentiles" (I Cor. 1:23). It is our task in this chapter to explore, with S. K., those obstacles to faith which are implicit in the very nature of Christianity.

Well-meaning interpreters of Christianity, eager to

make the gospel more palatable to themselves and others, have sought to select and emphasize only its more attractive elements. Here we find Kierkegaard's "wise and prudent man" who says:

> If only one could craftily get possession of His wisdom . . . without becoming His disciple! If one could slyly visit Him by night and get that out of Him—for I am man enough to draft and edit it, and in quite a different fashion, I assure you. (*Ibid.*, p. 47.)

There has been much of this editing. Ambitious and resourceful writers have come to "know" much about "the Jesus of history," and have reshaped his image into what they would like to have him be. They have used the nineteen hundred years of history to prove that Christ was an important historical figure, and on this basis have attempted to justify all that Christendom has become. They have become very knowing about Christ without being believers in Christ. They have substituted "knowledge" for faith, and history for the human problem and its remedy. They have, as S. K. puts it, eliminated the offense and made Christ "a divine Uncle George" (*ibid.*, p. 38). They have produced an idealized figure combining all the attractive elements of Ralph Waldo Emerson, Einstein, and Santa Claus.

It is therefore still our problem, as it was Kierkegaard's, to reintroduce Christianity into Christendom. The difference involved is the difference between poetry and reality—between applause and admiration on the one hand, and belief and commitment on the other. To become a Christian is to become contemporary with Christ. He is then no longer a mere historical figure, who some nineteen hundred years ago became the founder of a religion which is that of the Western world, and happens to be ours. When we accept our contemporaneity with him, he becomes the Absolute, and we can no longer regard him with historical detachment. We can accept or reject him; we cannot evade a choice. For faith, he becomes, quite uncompromisingly, "the way, and the truth, and the life" (John 14:6).

> Christianity did not come into the world . . . as an admirable example of the gentle art of consolation—but as *the absolute.* It is out of love God wills it so, but also it is *God* who wills it, and he wills what he will. He will not suffer himself to be transformed by men and be a nice . . . human God. He will transform men, and that he wills out of love. (*Ibid.,* p. 66.)

The Roman historian Tacitus describes the early Christians as haters of mankind. This has been widely believed to be a grossly misinformed description based upon hearsay and popular prejudice. It may not have been so badly informed as commentators have supposed. The early Christians renounced the world. They hated the world and its works. Christians are called upon to do this, and may, upon occasion, be required to hate father and mother for Christ's sake. God demands of us what he will, and one thing he clearly demands is that we accept and follow Christ, not on our own terms, but on his.

The Offensiveness of Christianity

Christ, who calls all men, saying, "Come to me, all who labor and are heavy-laden, and I will give you rest" (Matt. 11:28), did not expect that all men would heed his call. He foresaw that men would be offended by what he said and did, and by what he is. "Blessed is he," said Jesus, "who takes no offense at me." (Matt. 11:16.) The Gospels indicate various occasions on which men were "offended" (Greek, "scandalized") at Christ. His old friends and neighbors in Nazareth were offended when he spoke in the home synagogue and announced his Messianic mission. ("Who does he think he is, God?") The Pharisees were offended when Christ criticized their picayunish and mendacious legalism, and particularly were they scandalized by his saying concerning defilement— that it is not by what goes into the mouth that a man is defiled, but by what comes out. Many who had previously followed him were offended by his saying concerning eating his flesh and drinking his blood, and deserted him at that time. On the night in which he was betrayed, he told his disciples that all of them would be offended (RSV, "fall away") because of the events of that night. (The Scripture references cited are Matt. 13:57; 15:12; 17:27; John 6:61; and Matt. 26:31.) For his contemporaries there were numerous occasions of offense.

We shall miss Kierkegaard's point here unless we understand that we also are Christ's contemporaries. He is a living Lord who demands the allegiance of every man. As each individual human being is confronted by Christ's call, he must make his own choice. Either he will respond and become Christ's follower, or he will be offended.

> If thou canst not prevail upon thyself to become a Christian in the situation of contemporaneousness with him, or if he in the situation of contemporaneousness cannot move thee and draw thee to himself—then thou wilt never become a Christian. Thou mayest honor, praise, thank, and reward with all worldly goods him who maketh thee believe thou nevertheless art a Christian—but he deceiveth thee. . . .
>
> If thou canst not endure contemporaneousness, canst not endure the sight in reality, if thou art unable to go

out in the street and perceive that it is God in this horrible procession, and that this is thy case wert thou to fall down and worship him—then thou art not essentially a Christian. What thou hast to do, then, is unconditionally admit this to thyself, so that above all thou mayest preserve humility and fear and trembling with relation to what it means in truth to be a Christian. For that is the way thou must take to learn and to get training in fleeing to grace in such a wise that thou dost not take it in vain. Do not, for God's sake, repair to anyone to be "set at ease." For sure enough it was said, "Blessed are the eyes which see the things that ye see." . . . This was said solely and only about the contemporaries who had become believers. If the glory had been directly visible, so that everybody as a matter of course could see it, then it is false that Christ humbled himself and took upon him the form of a servant; it is superfluous to give warning against being offended, for how in the world could anybody be offended by glory attired in glory! . . . No, there was "nothing about him for the eye, no glamour that we should look upon him, no outward appearance that we should desire him" [Isa. 53:2, S.K.'s version]; directly there was nothing to be seen but a lonely man, who by signs and wonders and by affirming that he was God, continually posited the possibility of offense. A lowly man who thus expressed (1) what God understands by compassion . . . and (2) what God understands by man's misery, which in both cases is utterly different from what man's understanding is. (*Training in Christianity*, pp. 68–69.)

In other words, if I become a contemporary with Christ, and if I go out into the streets of Jerusalem and see the procession to the cross, I will know that, to worship and follow him, I must also be willing to suffer and die with him. This his own disciples, on the day of crucifixion, recoiled from doing. We also recoil, and in humility, in "fear and trembling," we become aware of what it means to be a Christian.

What the disciples saw in Christ was not a glory attractive to the eye. Popular Christian art in America has depicted Christ as handsome, virile, stern yet kindly, and distinctively Nordic. We do not know that any of these physical characteristics were visible in his face or form. Certainly he was Semitic, perhaps quite dark, and whatever it is about him by which he draws all men to himself, it is not pretty.

In him, in poverty, suffering, and lowliness, was revealed what God was willing to become in order that men might know what divine compassion is. Human compassion is willing to give and help in various kindly ways. Man's compassion, however, has its prudent limits. It does not motivate one to move from a forty-thousand-dollar home to a hovel, from suburb to slum, from comfort to deprivation, in order to share human misery. Nor do we invite the miserable to come and share our life with us; as S. K. says, "it would involve a change in all our household and manner of life" (*ibid.*, p. 12).

Furthermore, human misery as human beings understand it is not what God understands by human misery. Our deepest misery is not poverty, or hunger, or any physical suffering or lack; it is sin and the consequences of sin. God would not sin, and Christ is sinless; but God in Christ was willing to accept the consequences of sin in body and spirit by becoming a man, and by suffering upon the cross and dying as a malefactor. Men do not understand such love, and they are unwilling to accept it as true and real. It is contrary to the wisdom of human beings. To accept it would involve them in unwelcome self-revelation and demand a response in depth that they are unwilling to make.

This is the offensiveness of Christianity. It isn't a comfortable faith. But it is God's wise and loving provision for man's salvation.

THE OFFENSE OF BEING DIFFERENT

During most of Christ's ministry he was in conflict with the established order in religion.

> [Christ was] a teacher of godly fear and inwardness, who . . . with primitive spontaneity insists upon inwardness in contrast with all empty externalism, a teacher who transforms externalism into inwardness. Such is the collision, a collision which recurs again and again in Christendom. . . . The Pharisees and scribes here represent the established order, which precisely through their sophistry and shrewd wisdom had become empty externalism. (*Ibid.*, p. 87.)

Kierkegaard's discussion of this includes, as we might expect, a thinly disguised but obvious reference to his own conflict with the state church. In order to take Christianity seriously for himself, and make clear to his contemporaries what Christianity is, he found it necessary to challenge the caricature of Christianity which the established church represented. He was, as he well knew, an annoying, highly unappreciated gadfly.

Nor do churches today welcome gadflies. They are at best regarded as expendable nuisances by church official boards, presbyteries, district conferences, synods, and conventions. The latter represent official Christianity, and real Christianity is often in conflict with it. Few church boards or councils would be willing or regard it as "wise" to do what a genuine (and therefore radical) Christianity would call for. We are conservative and cautious, and Christ was not. We are orderly and legalistic; Christ was a fantastically free spirit. He was a preacher who had never been ordained, a physician without a license to practice, an interpreter of the Law who had not passed the bar examinations! He scorned the whole structure of carefully prescribed rules concerning food, Sabbath observance, and association with ceremonially unclean persons, whenever rules were in conflict with human values.

When we today view his life historically, we admire him for all this; after all, the Pharisees were "fuddy-duddies" and hypocrites. We forget that we also are Pharisees, and that, were he to come again in our time, we would be his critics, and after he had exhausted our patience, his enemies. We would not tolerate him any more than we tolerate Maurice McCrackin or Martin Luther King.

The church from the time of Constantine, Arius, and Athanasius has been like this. It burned Savonarola and John Hus at the stake. Its martyrs include Joan of Arc, William Tyndale, and Hugh Latimer. It ostracized George Fox and Roger Williams. John Wesley was not permitted to preach in the parish churches of the Anglican communion that had ordained him.

In the United States, religious diversity and legal safeguards have curbed overt intolerance and persecution. We still, however, find ways to persecute the free souls among us. We drop them from the official boards of our churches. Or we expel them from the ministry; we give them the little churches instead of the big ones; we ostracize them from normal, friendly social contacts. We close the platforms and pulpits of our colleges and universities to them, and deny them a hearing. We vilify them from the pulpit and in the press instead of finding out what it is they may have to say for the good of our souls.

This is not to say that every heretic or crackpot is a genuine representative of Christianity. Many such persons are mistaken, and most of them are socially and psychologically maladjusted. A few may represent dangerous errors. But often they witness to a truth, albeit a partial and distorted truth; and we will not listen. No one would contend that all "troublemakers" are authentic Christians witnessing to a truth, but official Christianity is never able to discriminate between the true and the false with imagination and insight. Therefore, to differ is to be wrong, and perhaps dangerous. Official Christianity, says Kierkegaard,

> would build up the established order, abolish God, and cow the individual into a mouse's hole—but this is what God will not have, and . . . he employs the individual to provoke the established order out of its self-complacency.
>
> When . . . the established order is deified, all fear and trembling are abolished. To live in, and more especially to attain, some position in the established order is a continuation of, or rather something safer than, hanging on to mother's apron strings—to such a degree safer that one can bank on the probability . . . of sure advancement straight into eternity. . . .
>
> And if with regard to this matter you encounter some obstacle, can you not be contented like all the others, when your last hour has come, to go well baled and crated in one of the large shipments which the established order sends straight through to heaven under its own seal and plainly addressed to "The Eternal Blessedness," with the assurance that you will be exactly as

well received and just as blessed as all the others? (*Ibid.*, pp. 91-92.)

Pretension, bigotry, and formalism characterize organized Christianity. Churchmen, bound by institutional apron strings, develop a spiritual myopia. They live in a narrow world bounded by the limits of their own near-sightedness. They become ecclesiasts, not Christians. We are all in this danger. It would be spiritually profitable for those who have any position in the councils of a denomination to turn deliberately and with open mind to the twenty-third chapter of Matthew, and read, from time to time, these words:

> Woe to you, scribes and Pharisees, hypocrites! for you build the tombs of the prophets and adorn the monuments of the righteous, saying, "If we had lived in the days of our fathers, we would not have taken part with them in shedding the blood of the prophets." Thus you witness against yourselves, that you are sons of those who murdered the prophets. Fill up, then, the measure of your fathers. You serpents, you brood of vipers, how are you to escape being sentenced to hell? Therefore I send you prophets and wise men and scribes, some of whom you will kill and crucify, and some you will scourge in your synagogues and persecute from town to town, that upon you may come all the righteous blood shed on earth, from the blood of innocent Abel to the blood of Zechariah the son of Barachiah, whom you murdered between the sanctuary and the altar. Truly, I say to you, all this will come upon this generation. (Matt. 23:29-36.)

THE OFFENSE OF BEING GOD

The offense of collision with the established order is rated by S. K. as minor. Far more serious is the offense to human reason of Christ's claim that he is Son of Man and Son of God. Consciously and deliberately he spoke and acted as though he were God. This claim of Christ's must be accepted by faith; it is not susceptible of proof or rational demonstration. Says Kierkegaard:

> Is it possible to conceive of a more foolish contradiction than that of wanting to *prove* . . . that an individual man is God? That an individual man . . . declares himself to be God, is indeed the "offense." . . . To "prove" is to demonstrate something to be the rational reality it is. Can one demonstrate that to be a rational reality which is at variance with reason? . . . The proofs which Scripture presents for Christ's divinity . . . are therefore only for faith, that is, they are not "proofs," they have no intention of proving that all this agrees perfectly with reason; on the contrary they would prove that it conflicts with reason and therefore is an object of faith. (*Training in Christianity,* pp. 28–29.)

That Christ was God *and* man is the basic paradox of Christianity; it is also the central truth of Christian faith. A paradox cannot be proved; it must be either accepted or rejected.

> If God exists, and consequently is distinguished by an infinite difference of quality from all that it means to be a man, then neither can I nor anybody else, by beginning with the assumption that he was a man, arrive in all eternity at the conclusion, "Therefore it was God." . . . The whole argument about consequences is incommensurable with the decision of the question whether it is God, and . . . this decisive question is presented to man in an entirely different form: whether he will believe that He is what He said He was; or whether he will not believe. (*Ibid.*, p. 31.)

The incarnation of God in Christ is a paradoxical truth that can never be converted into a common syllogism. To be understood, it must first be believed; but worldly wisdom seeks to approach it in the opposite way by trying to understand (i.e., explain) it first, and then believing it only if an explanation acceptable to reason is found. To many men today, even more than in "the days of his flesh," it is an offense to subordinate reason to faith. S. K. pictures a philosopher contemporary with Christ reasoning thus:

And the philosopher might say: "Such dreadful, or rather insane, vanity. For an individual man to want to be God is something hitherto unheard of. Never before has there been seen such an example of pure subjectivity. . . . He has no doctrine, no system, no fundamental knowledge; it is merely by detached aphoristic utterances, some bits of sententious wisdom, constantly repeated with variations, that He succeeds in dazzling the masses, for whom also He performs signs and wonders, so that they, instead of learning something and receiving instruction, come to believe in him, who continues in the most odious manner possible to force his subjectivity upon people. . . .

But even if one would overlook the madness revealed in the fact that *He* thinks himself to be God, it is an incomprehensible mistake, disclosing surely a lack of philosophic culture, to suppose that God could anyhow reveal himself in the form of a single individual. (*Ibid.,* pp. 51–52.)

The deity of Christ is still offensive to many "thinking men." The belief that he is merely a man appeared early in the history of the church, and has been a recurrent phenomenon. Particularly since the eighteenth century and the thought currents set in motion by the Enlightenment, men have sought to claim Christ as a human leader and teacher without accepting the "ancient superstition" of his deity. In the nineteenth and twentieth centuries, increasingly, science has obsessed men's minds with a standard of objectivity that seems to preclude the possibility of truth which cannot be demonstrated by scientific methods.

A recent sampling by *Time* magazine of the religious opinions of scientists reveals that the alleged return of scientists to religion has not been a return to what could, with any accuracy, be called Christianity. Although scientists are no longer scornful of religion, as were their counterparts a generation or two ago, the faith at which some of them seem to have arrived is an extremely cautious one. They are indeed appalled by the destructive potential of nuclear fission. They see that something more is needed in human life than mere knowledge if men are to live together in a global truce that even approximates peace. They are therefore more humble than the scientists of the nineteenth century. They no longer believe that "their questioning disciplines could eventually supply all answers"; but they find the churches "still too laden with ceremony and dogmatism for the scientific taste." ("Faith and the Scientist," *Time,* Vol. LXXIX, No. 26, June 29, 1962, p. 53.)

Scientists in general now have greater respect for the questions religion asks concerning the nature of life, the nature of man, and the meaning of human relationships and values. They stand in awe of the vastness and wonder of the universe. A physicist is quoted as saying, "I feel increasingly impressed by the great miracle that the world, so to say, exists. Its irregularities are as mysterious as its regularities." A microbiologist is also quoted in the *Time* report: "All good scientists stand in awe and wonder at creation. Only matter-of-fact scientists who are either inarticulate or brute mechanics might not have this sense of awe" (*ibid.*).

Some scientists have moved on from this sense of awe to full acceptance of a Biblical faith, and see no conflict between their scientific views and their Christian commitment. They find their understanding and love of God increased. Others find it necessary to leave creedal questions unanswered, and settle for the religion at hand, but with reservations.

> Religion, for many of them, becomes primarily a matter of being neighborly, providing good examples for children, or subscribing to a code of useful ethics. To James R. Dempsey, president of General Dynamics Astronautics, religion is primarily a matter of living up to the Golden Rule. "If this isn't enough," he says, "then I'm not going to make it." (*Ibid.*)

We should properly leave the question of whether or not Mr. Dempsey is "going to make it" to the judgment of a merciful God. It is proper, however, with complete respect for Mr. Dempsey's ethical religiousness, to point out that this is not the religion of the New Testament. Mr. Dempsey and many of his fellow scientists are offended by the full gospel of Christ. To believe in the reality of an omnipotent, omnipresent, loving God, to accept a living Christ as one's contemporary and make him the Master of one's life—these are things the doctrinaire scientist does not choose to do. To embrace and profess such a faith seems to him to be a violation of the scientific criteria of truth to which he is committed. He will not surrender his "intellectual integrity."

Science, as Kierkegaard points out, is an abstract approach to the problem of knowledge. It is in sharp contrast to immediate ways of knowing that characterize our day-to-day contacts with our environment and with other persons. Science dissects, analyzes, seeks causal factors. It investigates phenomena with ultimate purposes of description, prediction, and control. Science is objective; the scientist must eliminate himself as a person from his research. He is important only in the same sense that the adequacy of his equipment and the correctness and accuracy of his methods are important. His preferences must not be allowed to influence his observations or his conclusions. Like Sergeant Friday of the defunct TV drama *Dragnet,* the scientist "just wants the facts."

A fact is a correct and invariable relationship between an idea and an object. Since the ideas men have about things—the objects and processes of nature—do not always correspond to the objects and processes themselves, the work of the scientist is important. Not only are men's ideas grossly inaccurate at times, but there also are vast areas of actuality about which men are, as yet, almost completely ignorant. These areas of ignorance and mystery constitute the frontiers of science.

Even in science, the correspondence of thought with actuality is never complete, and scientific knowledge is always, to some degree, approximate and incomplete. Nineteenth-century scientists, in the first flush of success over their conquest of nature's mysteries, tended to overlook the limitations of their methods and the necessary incompleteness of their conclusions. They became obsessed with their own importance, and the public was overimpressed by their achievements. It was widely believed in Kierkegaard's time, and for a half century afterward, that science was the new key to all truth, and that in a relatively few years man would know everything!

It was, of course, a ridiculous conceit. It was of a piece

with the evolutionary optimism about man's future which has been shocked out of existence by the awful realities of recent history. Contemporary scientists, if they are thoughtful men, are also humble. They are aware of the vastness of their ignorance, and they are awed by the infinity and intricacy of the problems and processes with which they deal. Many of them, however, have not acquired a true perspective of their own frame of reference in relation to other, equally true, and perhaps more significant, frames of reference.

Science deals with means, not with ends. Insofar as facts are of such a nature that they can be acted upon, they themselves provide no motives for action or for choice between alternatives of action. Factual information can make clear the consequences of choice, and therefore serve as a very useful guide to making what men regard as the better choice. It can also indicate the kind of activity and the means to be used in order to attain the goals men may envision and desire. But the reasons and motives of men that impel them to desire, aspire, and choose are not in any sense scientific. Scientific method in the social sciences can, to be sure, discover and describe men's unconscious motives. The techniques of "motivation research" have been used in various manipulative ways to determine human choices and even to make drastic changes in personal orientation and values. Vance Packard and others have described these methods and indicated the dangers to personality and freedom that are involved in their use and misuse. (*Hidden Persuaders*, David McKay Company, Inc., 1957. See also Aldous Huxley, *Brave New World Revisited*, Chs. 7–9; Harper & Row, Publishers, Inc., 1958.) Science can, in many ways, be destructive of human values.

Values exist and are functional in a totally different

frame of reference. This frame of reference is subjective and personal, rather than objective and impersonal. It is concerned, rather than impartial. Indeed, its most typical quality is concern. This is the area of human life that Kierkegaard calls "existence." To exist is to be a free, self-aware, concerned human individual, living in meaningful relation to oneself and other selves. The existential individual is never self-satisfied. There is always a gap between what he is and what he wants to be. In consequence, he feels responsible for being more than he is. If he is aware of himself as a creature, he feels responsible to his Creator for being what his Creator means for him to be. This is, as S. K. indicates, a standard infinitely high. It is a standard of perfection, and man cannot attain it. It was to enable man, not necessarily to meet the standard, but to be freed from despair over his failure, that Christ came into the world.

Science cannot deal with this. It is the realm of the subjective—of relations between subject and subject, whether between self and itself, self and others, or self and God. Science is properly limited to the objective. The temptation to which the glorification of science exposes men is to objectify everything—to regard the scientific approach as the only valid approach to truth. Kierkegaard recognized this temptation as present and potent in mid-nineteenth-century thought. It constituted a temptation to which European intellectuals—even the clergy—were succumbing. They went beyond the limits of science in an effort to objectify and systematize everything.

The ideologies of the nineteenth century all professed to be "scientific," though any science worthy of the name would today emphatically disclaim them. The "Hegelianism" which S. K. denounced is now long dead. But the "Hegelian left" in the form of communism is still very much with us. What we may call "scientism," as distinguished from true science, is also with us; it is the attempt to extend the scientific way of looking at the world around us into areas of life where it can only obscure and distort the truth.

Esther Swenson has given us a capital illustration. She speaks of the serious error of "letting oneself be seduced into relating oneself to everything as if it were an object for scientific inquiry."

> One can take an example from the realm of vision. Suppose that one has a constant headache and an overwhelming feeling of fatigue and tension in relation to one's eyes. He goes to an oculist. After a thorough examination the doctor says, "There is nothing wrong with your eyes. It is simply that you have formed a habit of looking at everything as if it were as close to you as a book." Kierkegaard would say, "There is nothing wrong with the mediate mode of consciousness. There is nothing wrong with science. But there is something wrong with you. You have formed a habit of relating yourself to everything as if you were relating yourself to an object of science." ("The Crisis of Proclamation as Met by Søren Kierkegaard," *McCormick Quarterly*, Vol. XV, No. 4, May, 1962, p. 22.)

It is this habitual perspective of objectivity which foreshortens the possibilities of faith for many scientists and for millions of other people as well. Many intellectuals and many ordinary individuals have succumbed to a world view that blinds them to personal and spiritual realities. Their ears are closed to a whole realm of discourse in terms of which men communicate concerning the deepest meanings of life. This is why they are offended by Christian theology and particularly by the affirmation of evangelical Christianity that Christ is the Son of God.

Because scientific achievements have made a deep impact upon the thinking of Americans, there is a widespread scientism among us. It is an active ingredient in the "acids of modernity." All who are affected by it are offended by Christ's claim to deity. If they are in the church at all, and many of them are, they make peace with their consciences by accepting the gospel as "poetry." The typical "fuzziness" of popular thinking makes it possible for them to continue in the membership of our churches.

THE OFFENSE OF LOWLINESS

The difficulty of accepting Christ and the discipline of the narrow way is further complicated by the offense of lowliness. Earlier generations, beginning with the Gnostics of the second century, have been offended by the very thought that Christ was human, and have sought to explain it away by some evasive fiction. To contemporary Americans, Christ's humanity is, as such, no problem. They like to believe that he was a man like them in most ways, but better. They are even willing to accept the story of his sufferings at face value. They admire him for his unselfishness and courage. The more pious among them are willing to believe that he suffered in their behalf, and gladly interpret this to mean that his was a suffering to end all suffering.

Kierkegaard will not permit this easy interpretation of Christ's suffering humanity. To be sure, he suffered on men's behalf, and we are the beneficiaries of his loving willingness to do this. Christ, however, also made it clear that those who would benefit from his sacrificial life and death must be willing to become his followers. Every man must "take up his cross and follow" (Matt. 16:24). This is the offense of his lowliness, that we too are called upon to suffer; as he humbled himself, so we also must humble ourselves even to the point of happy and voluntary suffering—for his sake, and for the sake of others.

Kierkegaard makes a clear distinction between voluntary and involuntary suffering. More or less of involuntary suffering is the lot of every man. A Christian will accept involuntary suffering when it comes, and bear it with Christian courage and faith, but this is not Christian suffering. As S. K. says, pagans suffered misfortune and pain, and often bore them bravely, before Christianity came into the world. There is much misunderstanding of the nature of suffering even among the clergy.

> The decisive mark of Christian suffering is . . . that it is voluntary, and that it is *the possibility of offense for the sufferer*. We read of the apostles that they forsook all to follow Christ. So it was voluntary. Now there is a man in Christendom who is so unfortunate as to lose all that he possessed; he has not given up the least thing, he has lost all. So then the parson valiantly applies himself to study, or to whatever else it may be, everything is a confused buzz in the brain of His Reverence; to lose all and to give up all become synonymous, . . . notwithstanding that the difference is infinite. For when voluntarily I give up all, choosing danger and adversity, it is not possible to ignore the offense . . . which derives from responsibility when they say, "But why will you expose yourself to this and commence such an undertaking, when you could perfectly well leave it alone?" This is specific Christian suffering. It is a whole musical tone deeper than common human suffering. For when I lose all, there is no responsibility, and there is nothing for temptation to lay hold of. But in Christendom they have

entirely abolished the voluntary, and by this the possibility of offense as well. (*Training in Christianity*, p. 111.)

After we have made allowances for the sweeping nature of this indictment, we must acknowledge that what S. K. says about our confusion and our mediocrity in Christendom is essentially true: (1) We do not know what Christian suffering is; (2) we are offended by any demand that we be willing to suffer voluntarily; and (3) we regard a person who does make real sacrifices for Christ's sake as lacking in common good judgment.

A brief exposition of the meaning of Christian suffering, as Kierkegaard understands it, would go like this. Christian suffering is a corollary, a necessary concomitant of the experience of loving God. Love suffers in being separated from God by the distractions and busyness of life in the world. Yet the Christian is commanded to live in the world, and love is obedient. One who loves God desires earnestly to live a life pleasing to him. This would require perfection, and one does not achieve it. Always, therefore, one suffers from the tension between what he is and what he earnestly aspires to be.

Loving God, the Christian feels responsible for loving his fellowmen with a love that emulates God's love. But man is finite; he lacks capacity for an infinite love. And there are, indeed, some people whom he finds it extremely difficult to love at all. Even when a Christian does love his fellowmen with a love which in its finite way approximates divine love, men continually disappoint him and give him real cause to be anxious for them. New Testament examples of this human frustration of love are Christ's own lament over Jerusalem (Luke 19:41–44) and Paul's anxious concern for the foolish Galatians (Gal. 3:1; 4:19–20) and for his hardhearted fellow Jews (Rom. 9:1-3). It is part of the suffering of love that, as S. K. remarks, love is not always loved; sometimes "it is hated, ridiculed, spit on, crucified" (*For Self-examination*, p. 100).

The man who loves God will also suffer from the lack of any adequate means of expressing that love. Words prove inadequate, and worship seems empty. Loving concern for and service to one's fellowmen are imperfect and ineffectual. A Christian lives, therefore, in a continual state of tension—a tension made endurable only by his faith in God's love, wisdom, and power. There is much that he doesn't understand about the life which God gives him to live in this world. He is assured that someday he will understand even as he is fully understood. This, however, is an added suffering—the tension between what is and what is to be. Love must have, here also, the patience of faith.

This, basically, is what Kierkegaard means by *Christian* suffering. S. K. was himself a concerned man. He loved God; he loved the church; he loved Denmark; he loved his fellow Christians and his fellow Danes who were not Christians. He saw clearly the errors of thinking and the sins of heedlessness and arrogance that separated men from God and kept them from a full appropriation of the means of grace that God provided. In the writings of 1850-1851 he had plainly expressed his discerning judgment of the apostasy of his times. No one paid any attention to him. The "attack" was his last desperate effort to get men to listen, in the hope that they would in some measure respond. It was not a vindictive attack; its violence was due to the desperation of love.

Kierkegaard was also deeply convinced that his attack on Christendom was the culminating event in God's plan for his life. It was, he said, "governance" that moved him to do this. So he was willing to give all that he had, and all that he was, in order to confront men with the discrepancy between the Christianity of Christendom and true Christianity. He was willing to suffer the abuse and vilification that were heaped upon him by his opponents. He supported his publishing venture, *The Instant*, from his own fast-dwindling funds. On the day, October 2, 1855, on which he collapsed on a Copenhagen street and was taken to the Frederiks Hospital to die, he had withdrawn the last of his vanished fortune from the bank. He quite literally left all to follow Christ in the way he believed he was being led.

Who, in Protestant America, is willing to *suffer* for Christ? Who would not be offended by being called to lowliness and pain and sacrifice? Many of us follow Christ "at a distance" (Matt. 26:58)—and what a distance! It is easy to rationalize our reluctance by saying that Kierkegaard was an "exception," for this is, of course, true, as he himself said. But is it not possible that God is calling some of us to be exceptions? The way would be narrow and hard, and we are an undisciplined generation. We are mediocre Christians, and there is a reason for this. S. K. has a parable for our condition.

Once upon a time there was a rich man who brought from abroad, at an exorbitant price, a team of faultless and excellent horses which he wanted for his own pleasure and the pleasure of driving them himself.

A year or two passed by. If anyone who had known these horses in earlier days now saw them driven by their owner, he would not be able to recognize them. Their eyes had become dull and drowsy; their pace had no carriage and consistency. They could bear nothing;

they could endure nothing. The rich man could hardly drive them four miles without having to stop on the way, and sometimes they came to a standstill just when he was driving his best. Moreover, they had acquired all sorts of quirks and bad habits. Although they of course got food in abundance, they grew thinner day by day.

The rich man called in the king's coachman. He drove them for one month. At the end of the period there was no team of horses in the whole land which carried their heads so proudly, whose eyes were so fiery, whose pace was so beautiful. No other team of horses could hold out as they did, running even thirty miles in a stretch without stopping. How did this happen? It is easy to understand. The owner, who was no coachman and merely played the coachman, drove the horses according to the horses' conception of how they should be driven. The royal coachman drove them according to a coachman's conception of driving.

This is a picture of human life. When I think of myself and the countless people I have learned to know, I have often said to myself in sadness: "Here are capacities and powers and possibilities enough—but the driver is lacking." Through the long ages, for generation after generation, we human beings have been driven, if I may say so, according to the horses' conception of driving. We have been governed, trained, and educated according to man's conception of what it is to be a man. You see what has come from that—we lack spiritual stature. It follows from this again that we can endure so little, that we impatiently use the means of the moment, impatiently wait to see instantaneous rewards for our labors, which for this very reason become of secondary importance.

Once it was otherwise. There was a time when it pleased the Deity himself, if I may say so, to be the coachman, and he drove the horses according to a coachman's conception of what driving is. What was man not capable of then! (*Ibid.*, pp. 101–102.)

Kierkegaard speaks of the twelve apostles, gathered in the upper room after the ascension. They have lost everything, even the comforting presence of Christ himself.

And now they sit, cursed by the little nation to which they belong, and wait for the Spirit to be communicated to them in order that they may preach a doctrine which will raise the hatred of the whole world against them. This is their task. These twelve men are to transform the world—and under the most terrible condition—against its will. (*Ibid.*, p. 103.)

Kierkegaard could, I think, have cited other instances in Christian history when courageous, spiritually disciplined men, completely obedient to Christ, have done the will of God without being offended by the cost of discipleship or appalled by the magnitude of the task. This is not happening in Protestant America today. The way is narrow, and we are offended by narrowness.

CHAPTER EIGHT

A Faith for the Individual

FOR KIERKEGAARD, and, I think, for Christianity, man has no significance except as an individual. As soon as he is lost in a crowd, he ceases to be an individual, and loses his significance as a man. Said Kierkegaard: " 'The individual' is the category through which, in a religious respect, this age, all history, the human race as a whole, must pass." (*Point of View*, p. 128.) A crowd cannot take heaven, or eternal life, or the Kingdom of God, or Christianity, by storm. The entrance to all these distinctively Christian categories of existence is, as S. K. said, a "narrow defile." Or to use a different figure (mine, not S. K.'s), the entrance to life in the Christian sense is a turnstile, and the stern voice of God booms out over the loudspeakers: "One at a time, please!" This is not an arbitrary edict of God; there are understandable reasons why it must be thus and so.

" 'The individual,' " S. K. continues, "is the category of the spirit, of spiritual awakening." (*Ibid.*, 132.) And again: " 'The individual'—with this category the cause of Christianity stands or falls." (*Ibid.*, 134.)

> For one can guarantee to make a Christian of every man he can get to come under this category—insofar as one man can do this for another, or we may say rather, that he can vouch for it that such a man will become a Christian. As a single individual he is alone, alone in the whole world, alone before God. (*Ibid.*, p. 135.)

137

Only an individual man can believe, and become a man of faith; only an individual man can be offended and separate himself from God's forgiving grace. Always, Kierkegaard points out,

> offense is related to the individual. And therewith Christianity begins, by making every man an individual, an individual sinner. . . . Then it says to every individual, "Thou shalt believe," i.e., thou shalt either be offended or thou shalt believe. Not one word more. There is nothing more to add. "Now I have spoken," says God, "in eternity we shall speak together again. In the meanwhile thou canst do what thou wilt, but the Judgment is to come." (*Sickness Unto Death*, p. 253.)

Only the individual can be saved, only the individual can be responsible before God; only the individual will in eternity stand in judgment. Both in Kierkegaard's time and since, there has been a weasel-worded effort to "soft-pedal" New Testament teaching about the judgment. S. K. satirizes this very human attitude by comparing God's predicament to that of a civil magistrate faced with a situation of mob action in which the guilty are so numerous that it is impossible to place anyone on trial. Subconsciously, many an amiable Protestant reasons that, if there are so many of us engaged in sin, it cannot possibly be judged wrong or punished, even by God himself! As S. K.'s happy innkeeper remarked (in a different connection), "It's the big number does it!"

These wishful thinkers overlook the fact that before God as Judge, there is never a crowd, but only individuals. In the stark nakedness of whatever he is, each individual will come to judgment. "A man seated in a glass case is not put to such embarrassment as is a man in his transparency before God." (*Ibid.*, p. 255.) Not only in the "Last Judgment," but always and everywhere the individual is in God's presence. In a *Journal* entry, S. K. whimsically remarks that "the way in which people talk about God, . . . it seems to escape them . . . that God hears what they are saying." (*Journals*, p. 250.)

At least from the time of Jeremiah and Ezekiel, it has been clear that there is no collectivism in God's judgments. No man will be saved as a mere member of a nation, Israel, or of Christendom, or of any particular church. Men do not believe en masse, they do not love God en masse, and they are not transformed in heart and life en masse. Though corporate worship is standard practice in all churches, it is a vacuous formality except as one or more of the "worshipers" is truly worshiping.

It is true that man as sinner is "separated from God by a yawning qualitative abyss" (*Sickness Unto Death*, p. 253), but this is not the whole picture. Christianity is also a religion of love and mercy. Here, too, it is an individual faith. Every individual is the object of God's infinite, forgiving love. He is the beneficiary of the redemptive love and power revealed in Jesus Christ.

> For he is the friend of sinners. . . . He does not merely stand still, open his arms, and say, "Come hither"; no, he stands there and waits, as the father of the lost son waited, rather he does not stand and wait, he goes forth to seek, as the shepherd sought the lost sheep, as the woman sought the lost coin. He goes—yet no, he has gone, but infinitely farther than any shepherd or any woman; he went in sooth, the infinitely long way from being God to becoming man, and that way he went in search of sinners. (*Training in Christianity*, p. 20.)

Christianly understood, God's love has no meaning apart from God's judgment. To be sure, God did not send his Son into the world to condemn the world, but in order that, through him, the world, i.e., men, might be saved. We should not forget, however, that the world already stood condemned; men were lost in sin. Christ's redemptive act was necessitated, not by God's love alone, but in a context which included man's sin, God's condemnation, and man's total inability to conquer sin and escape his guilty condition.

In the Old Testament sacrificial system, the high priest on the Day of Atonement symbolically laid the sins of the nation upon the scapegoat, and sent him wandering into the wilderness. It was the goat's responsibility to get lost; and with him went the sins of the people. This system was a rather easy one, and would still be a great convenience for us all—if it worked. But it doesn't! Sins are not easily gotten rid of; and collective salvation is not effective.

Christianity is God's approach to every individual. And each must respond individually. Every man is to work out his own salvation "with fear and trembling" (Phil. 2:12). No one can fear and tremble *for* you! It is an awesome but inescapable responsibility that you must yourself will to believe, will to surrender and obey, and work out your own God-relationship in faith that God is working with you and in you.

As Kierkegaard often did, let us here become quite personal. You, "my reader," are an individual. You are aware of the mediocrity and hypocrisy of your own life as a Christian. Your problem is the same one that S. K. had faced in 1847: How does one become a Christian when he already is one? There is a way; S. K. found it, and dedicated the remainder of his career as an author to making the way clear to others.

DESPAIR AS THE BEGINNING OF FAITH

You must begin, not with hope, but in despair. The word has an odd sound in the context of shallow optimism that many accept as Christian faith. It is true that Christianity is a religion of hope, not of despair. But the only way to arrive at hope that is authentically Christian is by despairing of all other possible grounds for hope. So long as your hope is based on optimism about human nature, or the reliability of any human institution, or anything else human, it is not Christian hope, nor is it a justified or dependable hope. In the early years of this century there was, indeed, vast optimism about man. It is wholesome for Christian faith that the ostensible grounds for this optimism have disappeared. If you, in the 1960's, are trying to live by the escalator optimism of 1910, your hope is hopeless. You may, perhaps, be a Pollyanna or a Prometheus; you are not, in my judgment, an authentic Christian.

Civilization is a veneer. Underneath the mores and folkways that it imposes upon the individual is the same savage who roasted his enemy over the fire and ate him with uninhibited relish. A well-organized society restrains most men from crime; it does not prevent them from sinning. It can forbid murder, theft, and rape; it is powerless to forestall hatred, or covetousness, or lust. When the sanctions that society imposes become ineffective, or when, by some perverted ideology, a social group approves what decency has previously denounced, the natural man asserts himself. Then we get, not only the Nazi gas chambers, the Soviet gestapo, and the Chinese liquidation of landlords, but also horrifying juvenile crime in America.

This is not to say that social controls are useless, or that civilization has failed. Social order is a necessary framework for Christian living, and we are to "render therefore to Caesar the things that are Caesar's" (Matt. 22:21). However, the external controls that society can exercise are powerless to produce inwardness of character. Social controls at best foster an intelligent and cooperative conformity, and, of course, at their worst, a reluctant conformity. A Protestant church is a culture group which, as we have seen, engenders its own particular type of conformity. It was Kierkegaard's contention that the conformists to any social pattern, even that of Protestantism, are not real persons. They live in what he calls "unconscious despair" because they do not know who they are. They will never find themselves and achieve their destiny as human beings until they stop drifting with the currents of life that happen to surround them, and begin to be themselves.

Every human being is uniquely a spirit. As S. K. puts it: "The soulish-bodily synthesis in every man is planned with a view to being spirit, such is the building; but the man prefers to dwell in the cellar, that is, in the determinants of sensuousness." (*Sickness Unto Death*, p. 176.) What S. K. means is that man is endowed by God with the capacity to live as a spiritual being whose destiny and proper frame of reference are the perspective of eternity. Perversely, man prefers to neglect the upper level of his own house (the self) and live at the cellar level of the earthly and temporal. This is despair, for "despair is to lose the eternal" (*ibid.*, p. 185).

Your hope for becoming an authentic Christian begins, then, with the honest recognition that, up to now, you have lived in the despair of being like all the others. It is hopeful if you admit to yourself that you lack any inwardness of faith, that you have no real life of the spirit, no truly personal relationship to God, and therefore no authentic self. You may find it a difficult thing to do; but if you refuse to make this admission, you plunge back into despair, a deeper despair than before. For now you know your own emptiness. "The whole problem of the self . . . becomes a . . . blind door in the background of . . . [your] soul behind which there is nothing." (*Ibid.*, p. 189.) Your temptation here is to let pride prevent you from being honest with yourself and with God. Your prayer must be that God will make clear to you the seriousness of your condition, and that he will help you to discover and become the self he meant you to be.

If you can do this, you are from this point on an authentic self. You are, to be sure, "a babe in Christ," but you have become a Christian. This surrender of all pride is not easy, and many persons refuse to do it. They rebel; they refuse to be this honest, humble, penitent self; they try to construct instead another self. When a man does this it is an evidence of his unwillingness to be his real self.

> That blind door behind which there was nothing is in this case a real door, a door carefully locked to be sure, and behind it sits as it were the self and watches itself, employed in filling up time with not willing to be itself, and yet is self enough to love itself. (*Ibid.*, p. 196.)

Such an attitude Kierkegaard calls "the despair of weakness." If persisted in, and carried farther, it may lead to a hopeless state, "the despair of defiance," in which, instead of being unwilling to be oneself, a man wills to be a certain kind of self in rebellion against God. This was the hopeless condition of the scribes and

Pharisees whose frantic and fanatic opposition was described by Christ as the unforgivable sin.

To despair of oneself and of all human efforts to vanquish sin is to open one's life to God's love and power. But to fail to despair of oneself is to despair of eternity and of God. It is a failure to believe and trust God. It is to be a cellar dweller, obsessed by worldly, temporal attitudes and concerns in disregard of God's claim upon you and of his gift of eternal life. This latter idolatrous despair is what Kierkegaard calls "the sickness unto death."

Only a certain kind of despair is the beginning of hope. If you despair of God and do not trust him, you lose the eternal. If you despair of yourself and turn trustingly to God, you find yourself—and you find God. "The despair which is the passageway to faith is . . . by the aid of the eternal: by the aid of the eternal the self has courage to lose itself in order to gain itself." (*Ibid.*, p. 201.) This new life comes to you—or you come to it—by way of honesty, repentance, humility, surrender, courage, obedience, and faith.

FAITH AS THE END OF DESPAIR

All sin is despair in one of its unsaving and unsavory forms. *Sin* is an attitude of life which results in *sins*. Pride, thoughtlessness, and jealousy are, for example, such sins. If you would conquer these and other sins in your life, you must understand that all particular sins are but symptoms of that deeper, more pervasive sin—the sin of despair. We sin because we do not believe that eternal life is real and important, and because we do not trust God. We have an unspoken, surreptitious conviction that this life is all there is, and that our way is better than God's way.

The opposite of sin is not virtue, but faith. To believe that virtue is the opposite of faith leads either to frustration and renewed despair, or to Pharisaism (which is also despair). "Faith," says Kierkegaard, "is that the self in being itself and in willing to be itself is grounded transparently in God." (*Ibid.*, p. 213.) Faith involves this utter honesty, this willing transparency before God. It is a new relationship to God in which one abandons all posturing, all those stubborn and inane attempts at a childish and futile secretiveness.

The man of faith is humbly willing to be himself, i.e., willing to be the self God wills for him to be. In this relationship a man is freed from "bad faith" because he no longer is playing a role. Before God and his fellow-men he is what he is in all honesty. He will still know disappointment, discouragement, and frustration; he will experience "earthly despair" in the defeat of cherished concerns. But for the despair of eternity, which is "the sickness unto death," he has found and accepted the radical cure. Henceforth he walks with God.

THE CHRISTIAN INDIVIDUAL

Once you have set your feet on this way which is a walk with God, you will find that the life of faith is a many-faceted jewel of great price. Its struggles will be real and hard, and its sufferings many, but because of this its joys will be unexpected and rewarding. The jewel of faith will grow dim with your carelessness and neglect; it will grow bright with your faithfulness and diligence. Your life will become a rigorous but happy experience of being continuously tested.

To be a man, to live here in this world, is to be put on trial . . . , it is an examination. And the greatest examination a man has to take, an examination which involves one's whole life, is that of becoming and being a Christian. (*Training in Christianity*, pp. 181–182.)

Christ's whole life, S. K. points out, was an experience of testing, and he passed every test even up to the very end of death on a cross. The Christian life is a testing, not primarily of what one knows (though knowledge of the way is important), or of what one does (though appropriate action is essential), but of what one is. In this, as in any valid examining procedure, you who are being examined must give your own answers. Though Christians have fellowship together and help each other in numerous ways, no Christian can answer for another.

Christianity is in this sense a solitary way. Each of us stands in lowliness and loneliness before God. But there is help available. Says Kierkegaard: "There is abundant help and willingness in heaven; but it is invisible, so that . . . through it one may be helped to learn to go alone." (*Gospel of Suffering*, p. 9.) But even when the way is lonely and the going is rough, being a Christian individual is an exhilarating experience.

> For as the ship, at the same time that it is sailing easily before the wind, also plows its heavy course deep down in the trough of the sea: so also the Christian's way is easy when one looks at the faith which overcomes the world, but hard when one looks at the toilsome labor underlying this. (*Ibid.*, p. 6.)

The man of faith is a pilgrim in the sense that he knows that the satisfactions of this world, while often happy and meaningful, are never ultimate. As a Christian he lives usefully and worthily in the world, but his goal is to attain a heavenly city.

For faith means just that, that what I seek is not here, which is precisely the reason I believe it. Faith signifies precisely the deep, strong, blessed unrest which urges on the believer, so that he cannot find rest in this world. (*Ibid.*, p. 5.)

One of the great dangers of spiritual growth in our society is the noisiness and busyness and pressure of it all. S. K. thought it was bad in his day, and prescribes his own remedy for it:

When one considers the present state of the world and the whole of life, he is obliged Christianly to say . . . : It is diseased. If I were a doctor and someone asked, "What do you think must be done?" I would answer: "The first thing, the unconditional condition on which anything can be done, is: Silence! Bring about silence! God's Word cannot be heard. If, served by noisy mediators, it has to be shouted clamorously in order to be heard in the hubbub and racket, it does not remain God's Word. (*For Self-examination*, pp. 56–57.)

The word that God would speak to each of us does not come to us noisily. To receive him into our lives through faith, to know his will for our day-to-day living, and to know him better as the days and years pass, each of us needs some island of silence, our own citadel of quietness, separated from the hurry and din of the life that surges around us. This is hard to find, and no one can help you much with it—it's your problem. But if Robert E. Speer could find it daily in a twelve-minute subway ride to work, and if Brother Lawrence could find it among his pots and pans in the monastery kitchen, then there is good hope that you also can find it in your way. Certainly your faith must be nourished in some sort of quiet aloneness if it is to be an individual faith. Once yours and individual, it can be shared with your family, with friends, and with others. Until you have made it deeply yours you have little or nothing to share.

Faith and love combine in the Christian individual to give him that devotion to Christ which provides motive power for all that he is and does. It is in devotion to Christ that he finds himself. Said Kierkegaard: "It is true of man as of woman that devotion is the self, and that by devotion the self is acquired." (*Sickness Unto Death*, p. 184 [footnote].)

Always the Christian individual is a learner, a disciple. For him Christ is not only inspiration and power, he is also example. Humbly the disciple seeks, in his attitudes and relationships, to be an imitator of Christ. "Christ is the pattern, and to this corresponds imitation. There is only one true way of being a Christian—to be a disciple." (*Judge for Yourselves*, p. 215.)

To be like Christ is, of course, a counsel of perfection, an ideal impossible of full realization. All of us who seek to live in this way admit that we are followers who follow "at a distance." We are therefore continually humble and grateful that we are justified, not by our own performance, but by the authenticity of our faith in Christ. This does not excuse us from judging ourselves severely, as, says S. K., "eternity" will judge us. The faith that is in you will be searchingly examined as to

> how often you have won the victory over your own temper; what self-control you have exercised over yourself, or whether you have been a slave; . . . how often in self-abnegation you have been willing to sacrifice for a good cause, or whether you have never been willing; how frequently . . . you have forgiven your enemy, whether indeed seven times or seventy times seven; how

frequently in self-abnegation you have borne injuries patiently; what you have suffered, not for your own sake, for the sake of your own selfish purposes, but what in self-abnegation you have suffered for God's sake. (*Ibid.*, p. 13.)

Christ does not expect perfection in us; he forgives our human shortcomings. But he does require in us faith and love that inescapably express themselves in tangible ways. Each of us is called to a way of service that will be uniquely his own. Kierkegaard was very clear that the service to which God had summoned him was unique. He was an extraordinary contender for truth in his own time and situation. At the conclusion of Part I of *Training in Christianity,* he writes:

And what does all this mean? It means that everyone for himself, in quiet inwardness before God, shall humble himself before what it means in the strictest sense to be a Christian, admit candidly before God how it stands with him, so that he might yet accept the grace which is offered to everyone who is imperfect, that is, to everyone. And then no further; then for the rest let him attend to his work, be glad in it, love his wife, be glad in her, bring up his children with joyfulness, love his fellowmen, rejoice in life. If anything further is required of him, God will surely let him understand, and in such case will also help him further; for the terrible language of the Law is so terrifying because it seems as if it were left to man to hold fast to Christ by his own power, whereas in the language of love it is Christ that holds him fast. (P. 71.)

This is the relationship of faith—never perfect, and therefore relying humbly upon God's grace. Two things will the Christian individual watch carefully in himself.

One is that he will be completely honest that his life is only an approximation of Christianity. The other is that he must be sure that he is clear about the direction in which he is going. He seeks a life of the spirit, an eternal life, and a heavenly city. S. K. once remarked that it is "rare to see anyone write humbly about humility" (*Judge for Yourselves*, p. 134). There are many passages in his writings, however, in which he succeeds in making himself humbly clear.

> I say therefore also . . . that my Christianity is not the true Christianity, it is an approximation. Perhaps there are many in this case whose Christianity is an approximation. One ought, however, to be a little careful about this term "approximation," so as not to extend it so far as to include him whose Christianity is a departure from Christianity. It is so easy to make a mistake when on passing a man along the road to the city one does not notice whether he is going to or from the city. (*Ibid.*, p. 216.)

This, then, is the Christian individual—honest with himself, with God, and with others; penitent, humble, gratefully devoted to Christ. He has made his own peace with God, and he serves God and his fellowmen with loving self-discipline. He does not count himself to have attained, but he lives in faith. So Søren Kierkegaard lived; so he sought to encourage others to live; and so he prayed:

> Thou, who didst once wander on earth, leaving footprints which we should follow; thou, who still from thy heaven dost look down upon each wanderer, dost strengthen the weary, encourage the despondent, lead back the erring, comfort the striving; thou, who also at the end of days shalt return to judge whether each man

individually has followed thee: our God and our Savior, let thy example stand clearly before the eyes of our soul to disperse the mists; strengthen us that unfalteringly we may keep this before our eyes, that we by resembling and following thee may later find the way to the judgment, for it behooves every man to be brought to the judgment, oh, but also through thee to be brought to eternal happiness hereafter with thee. Amen. (*Gospel of Suffering,* p. 4.)

CHAPTER NINE

The Church on Earth

CLEARLY to understand Kierkegaard's perspective of the church, its nature and its future, is a baffling problem. His own relationship to the church, until the last few months of his life, was that of a devout layman. He had intended to become a priest, and had met all the educational requirements for ordination, but was never ordained because he became convinced that it was not God's will for him. Ordination and appointment to a parish would have given him "a living" and solved the financial problems that dogged him after 1848, but he scorned to do this. He could have become a country pastor and withdrawn from the arduous literary labors and the controversies in which he was involved, but this he later regarded as a temptation that he had resisted.

Comments in his *Journals* in earlier years indicate respect for and interest in the church as a historic institution. In one he noted that (1) the Greek Church evangelized several nations that later turned to Roman Christianity; and (2) that the line of church fathers continued in the Greek Church for 150 years longer than in the Western church. He whimsically remarks that the Greek Church had many fathers but few sons. In another comment he speaks of Faust who, as a literary figure, represents the individual emancipated from the church's guidance and left to himself, brilliant, but demonic in his desires, and moving inescapably toward his own damnation. Faust, said S. K., is a negative aspect and a parody on the individualism of the Reformation. Men, at least some men, need the authoritative guidance of the church. These comments indicate a perspective of two major functions of the church: evangelism; and Christian nurture and discipline. (*Journals,* pp. 43, 64.)

Except for a brief period of "going astray" in his youth, S. K. was a faithful attendant at the services of the cathedral Church of Our Lady in Copenhagen. From the beginning of his authorship in 1843, he had paralleled his pseudonymous books with the publication of "edifying discourses" under his own name, and after 1848, the discourses expressed his mature understanding of Christianity as a religion of redemptive power. Some of these "sermons in disguise" were delivered in Copenhagen churches. Though not ordained, he was an acceptable supply preacher.

In the last months of his life, he criticized the church with biting satire and bitter invective. His exaggeration of its faults was necessary, he believed, in order to draw men's attention to their seriousness. The late David F. Swenson remarked concerning Kierkegaard that "geniuses are born to us in order that mediocrities may have the opportunity to correct their errors" ("Introduction" to Eduard Geismar's *Lectures on the Religious Thought of Søren Kierkegaard,* p. xxiv; Augsburg Publishing House, 1937). It was not Kierkegaard's purpose to reform the church's form of government or theology. "Neither church nor doctrine," he said, "is to be reformed. If anything is to be done—then it is the reformation of us all." (*Journals,* p. 428.)

The only major change he proposes is the abolition of state support and control. Beyond this he hoped to make men see the gap between what the church is and what

Christ would have it be; see the yawning abyss which separates sinners (including each of us) from God; and see the urgent need for deepening the spiritual life of individual Christians. He called the church to repentance and a renewing of its life, and if his call is to be effective, this repentance and renewal must come in us who read his words. He is not recommending that Protestant churches establish a rule of celibacy for the clergy, or that a married minister desert wife and children for the sake of the Kingdom of God. He *is* earnestly suggesting that a minister and his wife prayerfully reorient their whole relationship to each other and to God in order that they may be more truly dedicated to his service.

He is not recommending that we drop from church rolls all who are lukewarm Christians. He is inciting us to an example of such faithfulness, such willingness to sacrifice and be sacrificed, that we shall "compel" others by the sheer moral force of our example to become followers rather than mere admirers of Christ. "Christianity," S. K. points out, "does not wish to compel anyone," i.e., by physical force. But it "wishes its followers to compel the world to become Christian by their sufferings" (*ibid.*, p. 428). If we find ourselves unable, presently, to live in this way, then we can at least pray for ourselves, and will feel too humbled to presume to reform the church.

The new reformation that the church needs is to be personal, spiritual, and charismatic, not ecclesiastical or dogmatic. The great doctrines of the church—the Fall of man, human depravity and helplessness, God's forgiving love, the incarnation of God in Christ, the redemptive death of Christ on the cross, the resurrection and glory and living presence of Christ, the availability of his forgiveness and sanctifying power for the life of the individual—all these were elements of the faith by which Søren Kierkegaard lived, and which he sought to make clear to men. There is here no heresy, but a dynamic orthodoxy.

Kierkegaard was not an enemy of the church. His criticisms were those of one who spoke from the inside, not from the stance of an aloof and condemnatory outsider. They were the "faithful wounds" of a friend who speaks out, not to despise or reject, but to voice a loving, even if querulous, concern.

It has been alleged by critics that it would be impossible to derive any constructive or adequate doctrine of the church from Kierkegaard's writings. This is the way he intended it to be. He was not trying to present a systematic theology of the church—an ecclesiology. He was calling the church to repentance. When we understand this, however, we can still sift some constructive and seminal ideas from the welter of satire and invective that we have been examining.

THE CHURCH IS GOD'S PLAN

Kierkegaard places himself in such irreconcilable opposition to the Danish Church that readers are likely to overlook the fact that he doesn't want to destroy it, but to shock it out of its lethargy. It would never have occurred to him that he could destroy the church. To be sure, he exhorted honest men to stay away from its worship services and thus cease to cooperate in "making a fool of God." This was intended as a warning against hypocrisy in worship, and also, perhaps, as a mass protest (like a one-day general strike) against the apostasy of the church. What he hoped for was acknowledgment from bishops and priests that their Christianity was not the Christianity of the New Testament. Though this acknowledgment did not come, S. K., in his last illness, felt that he had accomplished what God wanted him to do. He had witnessed for the truth. The outcome he could leave to God, and so he was at peace.

He was confident that the church would go on, and that the day would come when what he had written would be read and heeded, not just in Denmark, but by a much wider audience. Time has vindicated this confidence. The church does go on, and in many lands, including our own, is profoundly influenced by what Søren Kierkegaard wrote. It seems certain that he did not suggest or have in mind a widespread, "free-lance" Christianity outside the church, such as the contemporary movement in Japan, most recently described by Carl Michalson:

> Nonchurch Christianity in Japan is a movement seeking to foster Christian life through the Bible without participation in conventional church organization.
>
> The result for nonchurch Christianity is a strategy of evangelism; Japanese people gather in homes, schools, offices, factories, and farms to read and study the Bible. The methods of the teachers resemble Confucius more than they do Western ecclesiastics. People reluctant to enter a church because of its Western associations will gather around the Bible outside churches with no sense of restraint. The movement is often called "cross-legged Christianity" because of the way its followers sit about on straw mats, legs crossed in traditional Japanese fashion. Presumably Jesus also sat with his legs crossed as he talked with Mary and Martha and as he taught from a boat on Galilee. These historic allusions often conjure up the image of Jesus in the company of peasants. Nonchurch Christianity, however, embraces both peasants and university presidents in its membership. ("The Bible in Japanese Church Life,"

Bible Society Record, Vol. 107, No. 5, June, 1962, p. 68.)

Whether this is "nonchurch" Christianity or not is a matter of opinion. A good case can be made for the position that where a group of Christian believers are gathered together there is the church. The church has become an institution—a Western institution, if you will—but "Christianly speaking," it is a fellowship and a task force for evangelism and nurture; and both of these functions are being served by "cross-legged Christianity." Inevitably some organization is necessary to carrying on any program of this sort, and this will tend to crystallize into what we in the West call a church.

Was something of this sort what S. K. had in mind? No one can say with certainty; but there is no evidence to support an affirmative answer. My own opinion is that he would have wished these brothers well, but would not have found himself spiritually at home with them. He valued church order and the historic traditions of the church, and he valued the sacraments. He symbolized his return to Christianity in 1838 by coming to the sacrament of the Lord's Supper as a solitary penitent, and on his deathbed he longed for the Sacrament, but would not receive it at the hands of a priest of the established church. In this last period of his authorship, ten of his fifty-two published "discourses" are Communion addresses.

When the attack on Christendom was at its height, in August, 1855, S. K. published the last one of his discourses, prepared as always, as though for presentation to a church congregation. His publication of it at this time symbolized, I think, his continuing sense of membership in the community of grace which is the church.

He rarely mentions the church in his writings, but he takes it for granted always. He assumes it as a continuing body of true believers, the continuing agency for Christian witness and Christian nurture in a lost and needy world.

THE CHURCH NEEDS CONTINUOUS RENEWAL

The human leadership of the church is always imperfect and prone to error. Kierkegaard would have objected to my making use of church history to underscore this point, but I am unable to resist doing it. The church is indebted to a long line of reformers: Benedict, of Nursia; Wycliffe; Savonarola; Hus; Luther; Calvin; Loyola; Fox; Wesley—the list could be greatly extended, but such a list is illustrative of two correlative truths. One is that the church has at numerous times been blind to its own errors of omission and commission. The other is that God supplies a man for every such crisis. Church history is the history of alternating apostasy and reform. And always the perennial enemies of reform—lethargy and vested interest—are operative to prevent reformation if possible.

Kierkegaard did not think of himself as a reformer. He was a detective who had discovered a crime of the church against humanity, and was, by every means at his disposal, calling attention to his findings. He looked hopefully for a reformer, one who could lead the church in a return to the New Testament faith. S. K. was merely the forerunner of reform, a John the Baptist to its real leader. A hundred years have passed, and such a leader has not appeared; yet the reformation may be taking place in us and among us without the dramatic leadership of one man. It is just possible that the leader is among us and will be known only in the perspective of later generations of Christians. In any case, the need for renewal is present and great, and there are indications that in many sections of the church thoughtful Christians are aware of it.

It is a continuing tragedy that the Reformation which Protestants spell with a capital R resulted not only in reform but also in schism. Most previous reformations and some subsequent ones have taken place within the church, and caused no open break in relationships. All of them encountered opposition, and nearly all of them were the occasion for persecution by both church and state. Kierkegaard expected persecution, although in most countries of western Europe and in Protestant America, persecution has gone out of fashion since the Enlightenment.

Schism has also gone out of style, but denominational divisions that resulted from earlier schisms are still prominently with us. Even if, as Kierkegaard pointed out, Christianity is a paradoxical faith, to have 257 varieties of American Christians, each claiming truly to represent one Christ, seems a bit more paradoxical than necessary. There is now, of course, a strong ecumenical movement, seeking to discover some unity in the midst of our diversity, and seeking also to achieve the official reunion of church bodies long separated.

Kierkegaard would have viewed the official movements for reunion with skeptical detachment. As attempts to reform the church externally and organizationally, they would not have interested him much. His evaluation would have been: trying to add x units who are not Christian to y units who also are not Christian in order to be able to boast about $x + y$ units which still are not

Christian! It is the official hope, perhaps, that God will be dazzled by the big numbers, and will not notice the vacuity behind them!

The reform that the church needs, in our day and always, cannot be built into its superstructure by ecumenical architects; it must grow in the lives of Christians by the power of the Holy Spirit. Our need is for quality control rather than for corporation mergers. The church is apostate not because of its varieties of churches but because of a vast vacuum of faith and faithfulness. Reform must begin at the grass roots rather than by tinkering with the lawn machinery.

Our problem is that although God's grace is available, men do not avail themselves of it. Theirs is the despair of ignorance, in some cases of willful ignorance. Lulled by the tranquilizing effect of the pseudo-Christianity we have been examining in preceding chapters, they do not know their own need. It was S. K.'s conviction that:

> The need brings with it the nutriment, the thing sought is in the seeking which seeks it; faith, in the concern at not having faith; love in the concern at not loving. (*Christian Discourses,* pp. 248–249.)

God's grace is available; reformation and renewal in the church wait only for concerned men and women. When there is sufficient concern, the love, the faith, the transformation of attitudes and life, and the unity of the Spirit, which we now lack, will come by God's providence and God's power.

THE CHURCH ON EARTH IS THE CHURCH MILITANT

Kierkegaard's most constructive insight concerning the church is that on earth it can be only the church militant, never the church triumphant. His exposition of this thesis is a closely reasoned one. He begins his argument with a reference to Pilate's question in John 18:38: "What is truth?"

> Pilate's notion with regard to Christ was that Christ . . . was a man pretty much like the rest of them, and then only with his question seemed to single him out (untruly) as some kind of thinker . . . ; and he put the question to him rather in the role of the highly superior person who in reality looks down upon thinking as something which has no practical bearing, but takes pleasure in talking to the man for a moment in a tone of lofty condescension not unmixed with roguish jest— so it is that Pilate asks of Christ, "What is truth?" And Christ *is* the truth! Poor Pilate! There has been handed down that commiserating word of thine, "Look, what a man!" [Danish version of John 19:5.] But in view of thy question there is good reason to say of thee, "Look, what a fool! For this question of thine . . . is the most foolish and . . . the most confused question that ever was asked." (*Training in Christianity*, p. 200.)

Christ himself is the Truth, and Pilate did not recognize truth when it stood before him in the person of Christ. Here, in Christ, was true man, man as God intended him to be, the only completely authentic man who has ever lived. Here, also in Christ, was the truth about God, God who is willing to become man and to endure this pain and humiliation—to be a suffering Christ—in order to reveal his great love to men and make his grace available for man's salvation.

When it is Christ who is "the way, and the truth, and the life" (John 14:6), it becomes clear that Christian truth is not a doctrine or a teaching, but a way, a life to be lived. Truth consists, not in knowing the truth, but in being the truth. If truth were knowledge, then disciples might hope to go beyond their Master, and add to the truth, as for example, modern astronomers have gone beyond the knowledge of Copernicus and Galileo. But, says S. K., "It is different when truth is being, when it is 'the way.'" (*Ibid.*, p. 204.) The truth is something every disciple must live; it is something the church must strive to be in every generation. The achievement of one generation cannot be claimed by subsequent generations. Every individual and every generation starts upon the way just where all the others have—at the beginning—and is called upon to follow it to the end. Only when an individual has followed the way to the end of his life can he be said to be victorious. And only when the church has lived the truth—followed the way—to the end of time will it be the church triumphant. As Kierkegaard puts it:

> If a man will hold fast to this which is indeed Christ's own saying, that the truth is the way, he will perceive ever more clearly that a church triumphant in this world is a vain conceit, that in this world there can be . . . only a church militant. But the church militant is related to and feels itself drawn to Christ in lowliness; the church triumphant has taken the church of Christ in vain. To make this clear is the purpose of this argument, and it should be remembered that in speaking here of a triumphant church we mean a church which would triumph in this world, for it is entirely appropriate to speak of a church triumphant in eternity, corresponding to Christ's reception into glory. (*Ibid.*, pp. 204–205.)

S. K. points out three erroneous ideas about Christianity which have contributed to the mistaken belief that the church in this world can be the church triumphant.

One is the idea already discussed that Christian truth, like other truths, is a matter of knowledge. Christ's teaching is truth and is "an eternity higher than all systems, even than the very newest one [the "system" is Hegelianism], even than that which ten thousand years hence will be the newest; for his teaching is the truth, but in the sense that the truth is the way; as the God-man he himself is and remains the way" (*Training in Christianity*, p. 206). It is not wrong that men attempt to organize and systematize the teachings of Christianity, so long as these attempts are recognized, not as truth itself, but as signposts pointing to the truth. It should be remembered too that some signposts may not even point to the truth, but away from it. Men err when they regard truth in the Christian sense as something that is expressed by being verbalized, analyzed, or systematized.

A second source of error giving rise to the idea of a temporal church triumphant is the concept of Christendom, with which we have dealt throughout this book. When it is alleged that we are all Christians, then Christianity would seem indeed to have triumphed, and the church militant is no longer needed. It is an absurd error, but a dangerous one. It has well-nigh paralyzed the church, seriously impairing its sense of mission and urgency.

A third source of the erroneous idea of the church triumphant is implicit in human nature.

> Finally, this conceit of a triumphant church is connected with the human impatience which would lay hold in advance of what belongs later; and as it is almost universally observable that children and youth desire to experience by anticipation the whole of life, leaving nothing for manhood and old age, so has . . .

the human race, or Christendom, with like impatience
desired to anticipate eternity. . . . They would intro-
duce triumph within the temporal, which means to
abolish Christianity. . . . As soon as Christ's Kingdom
comes to terms with the world, Christianity is abolished.
If, on the other hand, Christ is the truth, his is truly
enough a Kingdom in this world, but not of this world,
that is to say, it is militant. (*Ibid.*, pp. 206–207.)

The true church is always at war with the world. If
ever it is assimiliated into society and becomes a mere
institution, a serviceable culture group, it ceases to be
the church. If it is to be the church at all, it must be
the church militant, and its battle with the evil forces
of this world will continue into the humanly foreseeable
future. There is little evidence that American Protestantism even faintly resembles the church militant. It
does not move "like a mighty army" in spite of the fact
that we often sing about it.

A student in a theological seminary has recently compared the church to a football team that loves its coach
so much that they give him a testimonial dinner, and
take up a collection to pay for covering the locker-room
floor with wall-to-wall carpeting, but neglect the one
thing he wants them to do—win games. (I am indebted
to Dr. Lewis A. Briner for this illustration.)

There is need in the church for both worship and warfare. The warfare is hopeless without the worship; and
the worship is meaningless without the warfare. Individuals must be disciplined and prepared for the fray,
for it is they who carry on the warfare. "And even though
the individuals were numbered by thousands and thus
were fighting in union, yet Christianly understood, it is
each individual who fights, and in addition to fighting in
union, he fights at the same time within himself." Neither

the individual in the world nor the church in the world can ever feel that it has won the war.

So long as this world lasts and the Christian church within it, it is a militant church, yet it has the promise that the gates of hell shall not prevail against it. But woe, woe to the Christian church if it would triumph in this world, for then it is not the church that triumphs, but the world has triumphed. Then the heterogeneity of Christianity and the world is done away with, the world has won, Christianity lost. Then Christ is no more the God-man, but only a distinguished man whose life is homogeneous with the development of the race. Then eternity is done away with, and the stage for the perfection of all is transferred to the temporal. Then the way of life is no longer strait, nor the gate narrow, nor are there few that find it; no, then the way is broad and the gate wide open—the gates of hell have prevailed, and many, yea, all find entrance. (*Training in Christianity*, p. 218.)

THE CHURCH'S TASK: CONFRONTATION AND DISCIPLINE

The major strategy of the church militant is to win by infiltration. There are undoubtedly battlefronts of social injustice where we must wage aggressive warfare; but the real victories of Christianity are won behind the battle lines, and inside the frontiers of the enemy; they are won inside human minds and wills. Christ claims the lives of *all* men, and calls them to *unconditional* surrender and commitment. This claim can be proclaimed from the pulpit, and before large groups of people. But a man can be confronted with the claim of Christ upon *his* life only in some kind of person-to-person contact that makes it impossible for him to maintain the anonymity possible as a member of a group. Revivalism—mass evangelism—may by the grace of God sometimes produce authentic conversions to Christianity. But this approach is a very unlikely and unpromising one if what we want is Christians who have committed themselves to Christ with real inwardness of faith and full knowledge of what they are doing.

Revivalism has been blamed for much of the superficiality and meaninglessness of membership in American Protestant churches. A recent report issued by one of our major denominations has put this appraisal quite succinctly. As the American principle of separation of church and state was implemented in the early years of our national life, and the abandonment of state support for churches became general, the weakness of the churches became evident. Revivalism was the answer to this weakness, and the churches that practiced it showed a steady growth in membership. Originally the revivalistic churches had "a strong ethical and social impulse," and standards were maintained, but during and after the Civil War there was a change.

> As revivalism became successful it led to a breakdown of standards for church membership and of church discipline. As more and more converts joined the churches, the problem of assimilating them got out of hand, and the churches began to reflect the society they had set out to convert. Consequently discipline declined along with commitment to the radical claims of the gospel. (*Church and State: What's at Issue?* p. 11; Board of Christian Education, The United Presbyterian Church U.S.A., 1962.)

This analysis is based on the work of Franklin H. Littell (*From State Church to Pluralism*, Anchor Book, Doubleday & Company, Inc., 1962), and its conclusions can, of course, be disputed. But it is a thesis that accounts both for the rapid growth in church membership since the late nineteenth century and for the superficiality of much that passes for Christianity in the membership of Protestant churches. It does not seem reasonable to expect that a faith which is individual and inward will be effectively communicated by mass methods. Crowd psychology and the manipulative methods and promotional claptrap that characterize contemporary revivalism are the farthest removed from Christianity. Except for the Holiness and fundamentalist sects, little reliance is placed upon revivalism by Protestant churches today. The Billy Graham campaigns, earnestly led by a man whose authentic faith is beyond question, are an isolated anachronism, the legacy of an era that is past. There is hope in the fact that the church has turned to other means of confronting men with the gospel.

The church is seeking and developing new ways to evangelize. A tremendous evangelistic opportunity is presented within its own membership. For outreach into the local community, visitation evangelism by two-member teams of laymen is a hopeful method. Its widespread use, however, encounters the problem that many team members are not authentic or informed Christians. It is difficult to see how they can communicate to others a faith which they do not have.

Kierkegaard would remind us that we should not "interfere" with another man's "God-relationship." We do not win men to Christ; we confront them with an opportunity and a challenge. It is the Holy Spirit, working through us and in them, who will move them to hear and heed Christ's call. More depends upon what those who work at this task *are,* than upon what they do or say, or how they say it.

The church has also a task, closely related to its evangelistic responsibility, of nurture and discipline. These are complementary terms. Without discipline, nurture is flaccid; and without nurture, discipline is repellent. Both are expressions of Christian concern for the spiritually immature.

The failure of our Christian education programs to produce literate and concerned Christians is due to numerous factors. It is certainly beyond the limitations of space and reader patience to attempt to analyze these factors here. Christian education has generally been carried on in our churches without much seriousness and with no severity. I am not advocating a "get tough" policy for church school teachers, but the setting of standards and adhering to them even if it reduces enrollment in church educational programs to a half or a tenth of the present figure. Children and young people have known that it would be all the same whether they learned anything or not. They know they will pass from grade to grade and be received into the communicant membership of the church without regard for their Christian attainments. Their parents also know this and most of them prefer it this way.

John R. Fry has recently taken what he calls *A Hard Look at Adult Christian Education* (The Westminster Press, 1961). It is an incisive and salutary book, and it would be equally salutary if Mr. Fry or someone of his ability would take a hard look at the Christian education of children and young people.

Church discipline is a forgotten phase of Protestant church life and a sinfully neglected responsibility. American Protestantism for a long time maintained a rigorous supervision over its members. Anyone familiar with the official records of local churches in the first half of the nineteenth century knows that exacting standards of conduct were imposed upon members. Erring members were summoned before church judicatories to explain their lapses, and often they were suspended from the sacraments until they gave evidence of repentance and reformation. Undoubtedly their Christianity was legalistic; sin was narrowly defined in terms of such things as drunkenness, profanity, lying, stealing, adultery, and Sabbath-breaking. There was strong emphasis on sins of the flesh, and failure to recognize the far more serious sins of the spirit. But at least the church was taking seriously its responsibility to guide, instruct, admonish, and encourage its members in a life worthy of the name Christian.

I am not proposing a return to an unloving censoriousness, but ministers and official boards of churches could exercise far more diligently than they do a loving concern for the moral and spiritual life of members, which would express itself in constructive admonition and counseling. Now we do nothing except, perhaps, to erase the name of the erring members from the roll, and usually we do not even bother to do this. So far as we are concerned, they can go to hell.

Historically, Methodism had a vital and useful supervisory device in its "class" system. If the entire membership of our churches could be gotten into groups of a dozen to fifteen, each with its "class leader," and with a program of prayer and instruction for the progressive sanctification of every individual, it would bring the "new reformation" the church so desperately needs. I am as deeply aware as anyone of the seeming impossibility of our being able to do anything of the sort. This is no reason at all for not trying, and any such small group we can bring together in any local church will be a step forward.

THE EARTHINESS OF THE CHURCH ON EARTH

When we have considered all the Kierkegaardian criticisms of the church, when we have painstakingly noted the church's manifest faults and errors, its missed opportunities, and its divergence from the Christianity of the New Testament, there is one thing more that must be said before we bring this chapter—and this book—to a close. The church on earth is *necessarily* human. This seemingly obvious statement can be understood to have a double meaning, and both meanings are intended.

First, it is *unavoidable* that the church will be human, very human. It is composed of human beings, and it ministers to human needs. It will take on in every society something of the protective coloration appropriate to that society. It is a *social* institution. What Kierkegaard objected to was that the Danish Church had lost its separateness and had become merely a social institution. As we have seen, this also is happening to the Protestant churches in America.

The church cannot avoid its humanity or its human weaknesses. The New Testament church was very human. Recurrently in the book of The Acts and in the situations that lie back of the epistles, the vagaries and weaknesses of human nature appear. Some Christians were merely ill informed and undisciplined. Some, like Simon Magus, were obviously bent on exploiting Christianity rather than on serving it. There were hypocrites like Ananias and Sapphira, and still others like the unnamed individual in Corinth who was flagrantly living in an adulterous relationship with his father's wife.

The church has never been perfect. This does not mean that we should accept its imperfections complacently. It does mean that we should accept them honestly, and without cynicism or despair. It means that we should labor the more earnestly to make the church more nearly worthy to be the body of Christ and the instrument of his redemptive purpose.

Secondly, it is not only unavoidable, it is *essential* that the church be human. As Christ was divine and human, so must his church be. The incarnation was necessary because the old covenant of the Law did not communicate God's love to men or mediate his reconciling grace. The church is in the world as an agency of communication and reconciliation. But to a considerable extent today it fails to communicate to men any saving awareness of God's judgment and God's grace. We have observed that the church is too involved in the culture of our time and nation to be at all clear about what it has to communicate.

There is an opposite danger, and paradoxically, it is a real and present one. Christianity tends to be a Sunday religion in our time because it is so usually expressed in a Sunday language. Its meanings and behavior patterns are understood in terms of an archaic tradition, and its message is couched in dull irrelevancies. Rudolf Bultmann's now well-known proposal for "demythologizing the gospel" would devise a new language for the communication of Christian truth. ("New Testament and Mythology," in H. W. Bartsch, ed., *Kerygma and Myth;* Society for the Propagation of Christian Knowledge, London, 1953.) To reveal Christ with contemporaneity to our generation is undoubtedly an important and difficult problem. Bultmann has erred, I think, in assuming that the gospel can be divorced from the "mythos" in which it was originally expressed without losing something that is essential to the gospel. He has erred even more seriously in supposing that the problem of communicating the gospel is primarily verbal. This is part of it, indeed, but neither the whole nor the heart of it. The problem is not what to say about Christ or how to say it, but what to do, how to live, so that we may make clear to others what Christ means.

The young martyr Dietrich Bonhoeffer had, in this respect, the right idea, and an opportunity to demonstrate it. His experiences in a Nazi prison, and his courage in meeting death for Christ's sake, rise to the level of *being* the truth as few men have done in our time. It does not detract from Bonhoeffer's achievement to say, however, that, given equal faith and courage, it is a simpler matter to know how to be the truth in the face of pagan Nazi brutality than to know how to make one's life equally true in the midst of pseudo-Christian mediocrity. This is the problem of concerned Christians in American churches. Its solution calls for intelligent and incisive thinkers who will point out the ways in which we are to live the Way; it calls also for courageous exemplars who will live the Way in these ways. There are tasks and challenges here that go beyond Kierkegaard—as he would want us to do.

Paul's observation that "we have this treasure in earthen vessels" (II Cor. 4:7) has recently been made the thesis of an insightful sociological study by James M. Gustafson. The church's "human social character is essential to its purposes," says Dr. Gustafson. Its humble humanness and its weakness are not misfortunes. The church on earth is not here for the purpose of being exalted. It must not become such an object of adoration that, quite unrealistically indeed, we make it a fourth member of the Godhead. Its "power and effectiveness depend upon its humanity, even its sinful humanity."

> Because it is a *human community* the church can make Christ present to men. Its social adaptiveness is a strength rather than a weakness, a good rather than an evil. It must find the political forms, patterns of interpretation, and liturgies through which Christ can make himself present to the disinherited Negroes and Puerto Ricans of Manhattan, the Hindu Tamils of Ceylon, the dying aristocracy of western Europe, and the people of eastern Europe under Soviet domination. (*Treasure in Earthen Vessels: The Church as a Human Community,* p. 111; Harper & Row, Publishers, Inc., 1961.)

Social adaptiveness has always been characteristic of the church, and is not itself a sin. It becomes sinful, as Kierkegaard sought to show, when the essential truth for which the church is to witness is lost in social adaptiveness. We live in a time of multiple and complex tensions, but this is not new for the church. It has always lived in tension with society. It has also lived with numerous other tensions, including the tension that it never measures up to its own image of itself. It is never what it ought to be—what Christ would have it be.

Even if it were perfect, the church in the world would always have its critics and its enemies. We should expect this and welcome it. The enemies of the church are strong in the world today. It is not these external enemies, communist or others, who are the greatest danger to the church. Nor is it our greatest danger that the church has to some extent adapted itself to the society of which it is a part. Our greatest danger is still the one which has been the burden of this book, that the church has gone so far in the direction of becoming a merely human social institution that it is losing its separateness, and in losing its separateness it will lose itself.

Our most serious cause for alarm is not our enemies, but our friends who speak so well of us.

Selected Bibliography

Except as otherwise noted, all Scripture quotations are from the Revised Standard Version of the Holy Bible, and are used by permission of the National Council of Churches.

The following books by Søren Kierkegaard have been used and quoted in the present work. All but two of them were written in the last period of his authorship. The exceptions are the *Concluding Unscientific Postscript* (1845) and *The Journals*, which represent the miscellaneous thoughts of twenty years (1834–1854) of S. K.'s life. I hope that many readers will be moved to read Kierkegaard for themselves. None of the works written in the last period, 1848–1855, is difficult to read with the possible exception of *The Sickness Unto Death*. All of them are searchingly and helpfully devotional, though some readers will not find the polemicism of the *Attack* devotional in the ordinary sense of the word. *Training in Christianity* is the most direct statement of the Christianity of the individual. For those who desire the most modest beginning possible, the paperback edition of *For Self-examination* is recommended.

Where more than one edition of a book is listed, the first mentioned is the edition from which I have quoted.

Attack Upon "Christendom," tr. by Walter Lowrie. A Beacon Paperback, Beacon Press, Inc., 1956. Original U.S. edition, Princeton University Press, 1944.

Christian Discourses with *The Lilies of the Field* and *Three Discourses at the Communion on Fridays*, tr. by Walter Lowrie. Oxford University Press (London), 1939.

Concluding Unscientific Postscript, tr. by David F. Swenson and Walter Lowrie. Princeton University Press, 1941.

For Self-examination, tr. by Edna and Howard Hong. Augsburg Publishing House, 1940 (Paperback). Also published with *Judge for Yourselves!* tr. by Walter Lowrie. Princeton University Press, 1944.

The Gospel of Suffering, tr. by David F. and Lillian Marvin Swenson. Augsburg Publishing House, 1948.

The Journals of Søren Kierkegaard, ed. and tr. by Alexander Dru. Oxford University Press (London), 1938. Also published as Torchbook TB 52, Harper & Row, Publishers, Inc., 1959.

Judge for Yourselves! (with *For Self-examination*), tr. by Walter Lowrie. Princeton University Press, 1944.

The Point of View for My Work as an Author: A Report to History, tr. by Walter Lowrie, ed. by Benjamin Nelson. Torchbook TB 88, Harper & Row, Publishers, Inc., 1962. Originally published in English (with *Two Notes About "The Individual"* and *On My Work as an Author*) by Oxford University Press, Inc., 1939.

Purity of Heart, tr. by Douglas V. Steere. Harper & Row, Publishers, Inc., 1938. Also published by Alec R. Allenson, Inc., 1948; and as Torchbook TB 4, Harper & Row, Publishers, Inc., 1956.

The Sickness Unto Death (with *Fear and Trembling*), tr. by Walter Lowrie. Anchor Book, Doubleday & Company, Inc., 1954. Originally published in English by Princeton University Press, 1941.

Training in Christianity, tr. by Walter Lowrie. Princeton University Press, 1944.